BLACK VOICES

INSPIRING & EMPOWERING QUOTES FROM GLOBAL THOUGHT LEADERS

Jessica Ann Mitchell Aiwuyor

global

CONTENTS

INTRODUCTION

From African griots to modern-day historians, recognizing the power of the spoken and written word is a time-honored tradition in the Pan African world. Through the "word," we honor our history, and through the "word," we build our future. The *Black Voices* collection explores speeches, interviews, writings, and sayings of people of African descent worldwide. The Pan African world includes people from the continent of Africa and descendants of Africans who were dispersed globally, mainly due to the transatlantic slave trade.

These descendants are commonly referred to as the African diaspora. An estimated twelve million Africans were enslaved and forcibly displaced during the trade. Despite centuries of displacement and oppression, descendants of Africans continue to make our presence known and are celebrated globally. Despite oppressive attempts at erasure, the African diaspora retained various aspects of our ancestors' heritages and created new cultural identities and traditions. Our influences can be witnessed through many countries' food, music, language, and practices.

For centuries, the African diaspora and the overall Pan African world have used culture, creativity, and ingenuity to protect our communities and forge new paths for future generations. The Pan African world is expansive and diverse but shares cultural bonds that have endured over time. We have also bonded over the shared goal of ending anti-Black racism and oppression within our native countries and internationally.

The words of the Pan African collective have been used to positively influence lives, communities, nations, and the world. Our voices are more than words; they are tools for chain-breaking and movement-building. Through literature, we used the art of storytelling to preserve our cultural memories, explored new possibilities, and became empowered.

Through art, we showcased the beauty and depth of our communities. Through activism, we became the change we wanted to see, pressed forward, and demanded civil and human rights to ensure a more just and equitable world. Thus, the African diaspora has consistently included trendsetters, world makers, and advocates for change. Through love, we envisioned and worked toward a world of freedom and a world in which our families and communities could thrive. Through Pan Africanism, we struggled together, and we unified and uplifted the collective Pan African world for the benefit of us all.

The *Black Voices* collection of quotes showcases the various voices of African descendants, including African, African American, Afro-Caribbean, Black European, Black British, and Afro-Latino thought leaders—along with valuable lesser-known voices that are impactful, inspiring, and diverse. *Black Voices* includes thought-provoking and endearing quotes on culture and history, love, womanhood and girlhood, activism, education, Pan Africanism, politics, liberation, inspiration, race, and Blackness. Additionally, *Black Voices* includes old and contemporary voices, leaning on our ancestors' works while recognizing our elders' accomplishments and uplifting rising thought leaders. I hope this collection of insightful quotes from the Pan African world will help preserve our cultural legacy and inspire the next generation to fulfill their destiny.

CULTURE AND HISTORY

History and culture represent the heartbeat of the Pan African world. For Africans and African descendants in the diaspora, history serves as a guide for pride, education, self-preservation, identity, and self-love. From our history, we learn our roots. From our history, we understand the struggles and triumphs of our ancestors and use their past as motivation for our future. Culture serves as nourishment for our souls. Culture is what moves us and shapes our worldview. Culture is what informs collective knowledge, needs, and desires. It is through culture that we embrace the robustness of our heritage and true selves.

For centuries, during periods of enslavement and colonialism, our histories and cultures were suppressed. Many of our ancestors had to hide our stories inside themselves or face punishment or backlash. In the Americas, African descendants had to gather at night to tell stories, share information, pass down multigenerational knowledge, and worship the deities of their choice. Throughout African history, our stories were documented both orally and through the written word. During the dispersal of the African diaspora (also known as the Maafa, a Swahili word meaning "great tragedy"), our ancestors planted their truths within themselves by preserving and passing along Africanisms. Through the centuries these Africanisms, remnants of various African ethnicities, still show themselves through our music, speech, foods, hairstyles, clothing, poetry, art, and more. This is culture and the memories preserving them are our history.

The following sequence of quotes features insightful Africans and African descendants, reflecting on the power and strength of history and culture, and how they can be used for understanding and empowerment.

artist | Erin K. Robinson, *Dada Wazuri*

Arturo Alfonso Schomburg (1884–1938) was a bibliophile, scholar, and namesake of the Schomburg Center for Research in Black Culture in New York. He was born in Puerto Rico but later moved to the United States, where he collected a vast reservoir of cultural and historical information and artifacts about Black people in the Americas. Schomburg is credited with preserving African American, Afro-Latino, and Afro-diasporic cultural history, information, and artifacts. He was also a member of the scholar-activist organization the American Negro Academy (ANA).

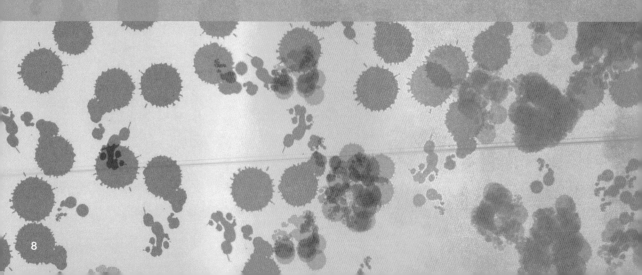

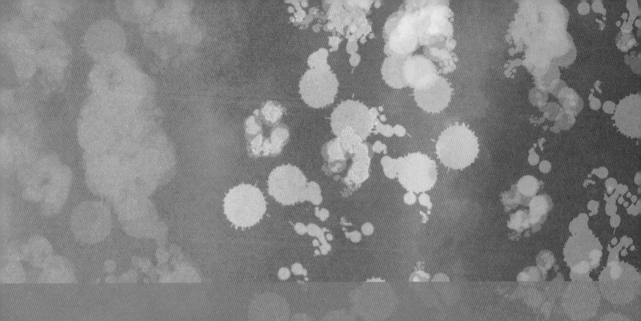

"We need the historian and philosopher to give us with trenchant pen, the story of our forefathers, and let our soul and body, with phosphorescent light, brighten the chasm that separates us. We should cling to them just as blood is thicker than water."

Arturo Alfonso Schomburg, Afro–Puerto Rican historian

Dr. John Henrik Clarke (1915–1998) was known widely as a leader of African-centered education. He was a lecturer, biographer, historian, journalist, novelist, and scholar-activist. He was a key figure in the African-centered Education Movement. Clarke also wrote the Social Studies/History section in the Geocultural Baseline Essay series, commissioned by the public school district of Portland, Oregon, which was one of the earliest efforts to develop and implement a multicultural and multiethnic curriculum as a national model for the United States' public school system. Dr. Clarke was professor emeritus of African world history at the Department of Africana and Puerto Rican Studies at Hunter College, part of the City University in New York.

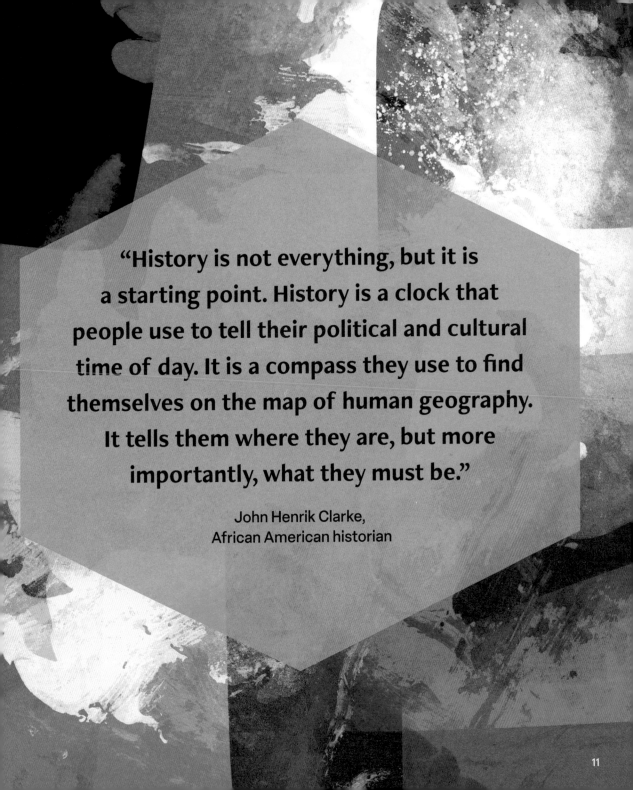

"History is not everything, but it is a starting point. History is a clock that people use to tell their political and cultural time of day. It is a compass they use to find themselves on the map of human geography. It tells them where they are, but more importantly, what they must be."

John Henrik Clarke,
African American historian

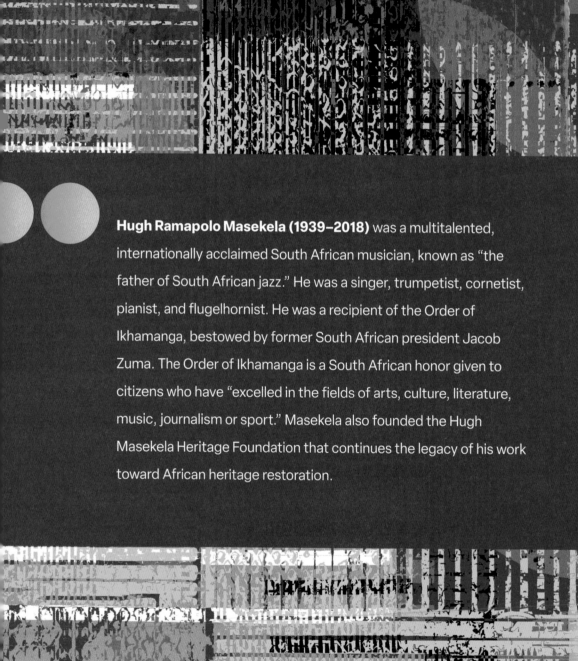

Hugh Ramapolo Masekela (1939–2018) was a multitalented, internationally acclaimed South African musician, known as "the father of South African jazz." He was a singer, trumpetist, cornetist, pianist, and flugelhornist. He was a recipient of the Order of Ikhamanga, bestowed by former South African president Jacob Zuma. The Order of Ikhamanga is a South African honor given to citizens who have "excelled in the fields of arts, culture, literature, music, journalism or sport." Masekela also founded the Hugh Masekela Heritage Foundation that continues the legacy of his work toward African heritage restoration.

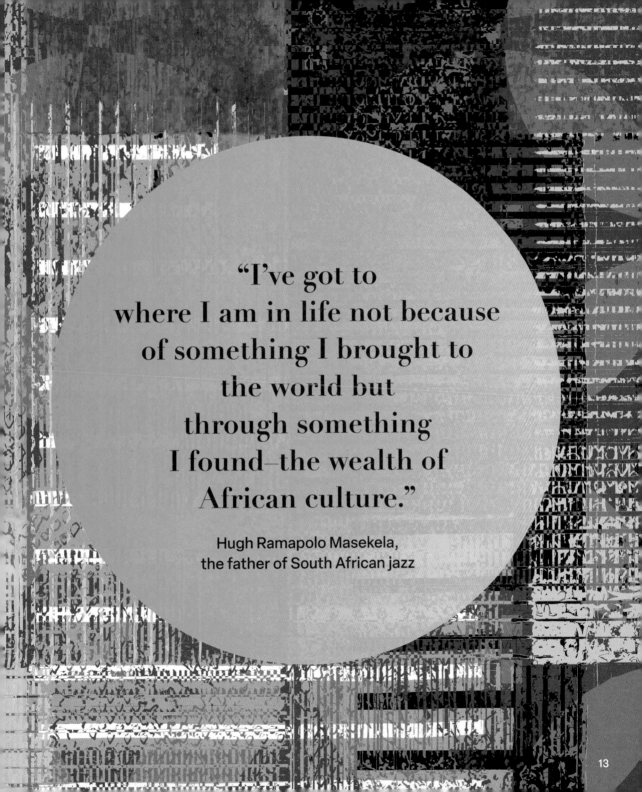

"I've got to
where I am in life not because
of something I brought to
the world but
through something
I found–the wealth of
African culture."

Hugh Ramapolo Masekela,
the father of South African jazz

13

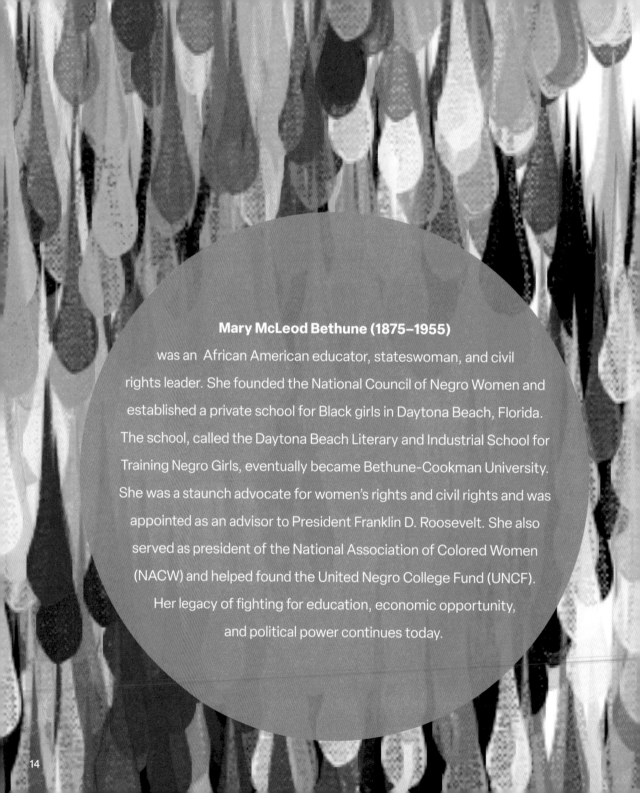

Mary McLeod Bethune (1875–1955)

was an African American educator, stateswoman, and civil rights leader. She founded the National Council of Negro Women and established a private school for Black girls in Daytona Beach, Florida. The school, called the Daytona Beach Literary and Industrial School for Training Negro Girls, eventually became Bethune-Cookman University. She was a staunch advocate for women's rights and civil rights and was appointed as an advisor to President Franklin D. Roosevelt. She also served as president of the National Association of Colored Women (NACW) and helped found the United Negro College Fund (UNCF). Her legacy of fighting for education, economic opportunity, and political power continues today.

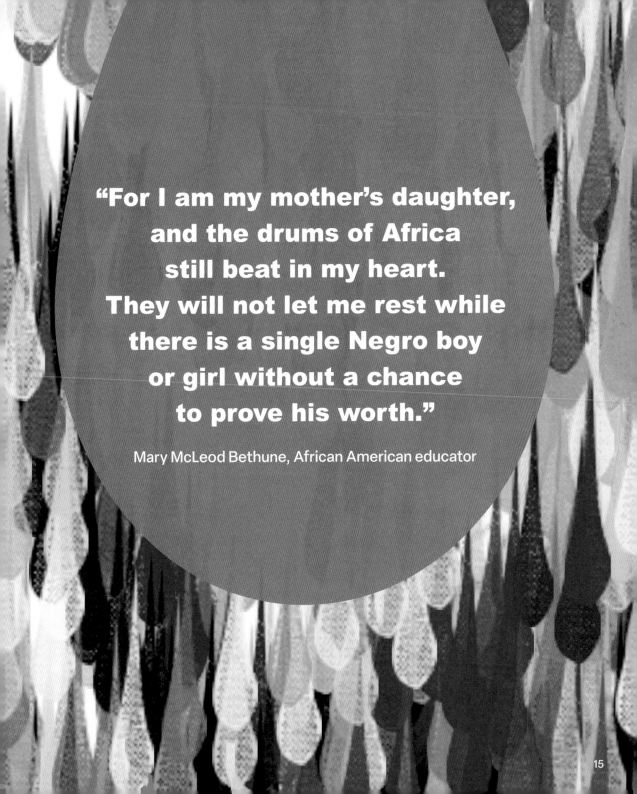

"For I am my mother's daughter,
and the drums of Africa
still beat in my heart.
They will not let me rest while
there is a single Negro boy
or girl without a chance
to prove his worth."

Mary McLeod Bethune, African American educator

Dr. Marta Morena Vega (b. 1942), born in East Harlem, New York, is a leading Afro–Puerto Rican educator, activist, and cultural ambassador. Her works focus on creating institutions for people of African descent on the international stage. As founder of the Caribbean Cultural Center African Diaspora Institute (CCCADI), Dr. Vega's work is centered on "assuring that the contributions of African and African descendants are integral to the lives of civil society in the Americas." Dr. Vega also founded the Association of Hispanic Arts. She is the chief editor of *Women Warriors of the Afro-Latina Diaspora* (2012) and author of *The Altar of My Soul* (2001). Additionally, she was the director and co-producer of the documentary *When the Spirits Dance Mambo: Growing Up Nuyorican in El Barrio* (2003).

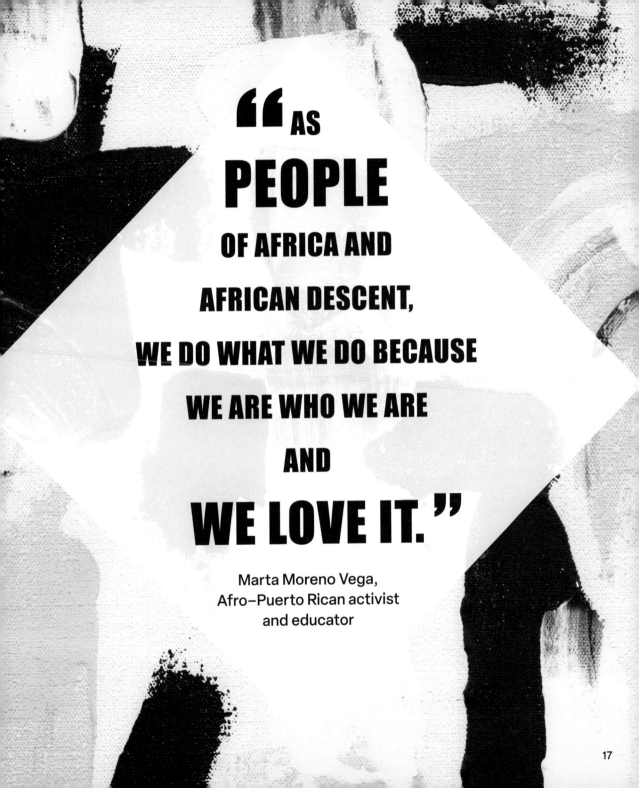

" AS PEOPLE OF AFRICA AND AFRICAN DESCENT, WE DO WHAT WE DO BECAUSE WE ARE WHO WE ARE AND WE LOVE IT. "

Marta Moreno Vega,
Afro-Puerto Rican activist
and educator

Werewere Liking (b. 1950) is a Cameroonian-born author and playwright from the Bassa people currently residing in Abidjan, Côte d'Ivoire. She is a groundbreaking and leading Francophone African woman writer, known for works exploring African culture, identity, and traditions. She is also a Pan Africanist, believing in the interconnection of the Pan African world. Her artistry is extensive, and includes writing, poetry, puppetry, dance, singing, and playwriting. In 2000, she was awarded the Prince Claus Award, which is granted by the Netherlands and aims to support artists residing in countries where "culture is under pressure." She also won the acclaimed Noma Award for Publishing in Africa for her novel *La mémoire amputée* (*The Amputated Memory*, 2004) in 2005. She is the founder of Ki-Yi village, an independent multinational cooperative of artists and performers based in the Village Ki-Yi M'Bock Center for Cultural Exchange.

"I come from a culture where the role of the artist is not very different from that of the priest. For the one and for the other (the artist and the priest), it's all about leading others to the contemplation and elevation of the soul, in its aspirations to strive toward the infinity of the divine, toward beauty and pleasure, toward being and knowing, but, to put it more simply, it's also about tolerance and harmony in our daily existence, about motivation and dissuasion, about business and pleasure."

Werewere Liking, Cameroonian author

Olaudah Equiano (ca. 1745–1797) was a West African (from Igboland, in modern-day Nigeria) writer, sailor, merchant, and prominent abolitionist who lived during the eighteenth century. He is most widely known as the author of *The Interesting Narrative of the Life of Olaudah Equiano, or Gustava Vassa the African, Written by Himself* (1789), considered one of the most complete accounts of the transatlantic slave trade and an indispensable document for the final abolition of slavery in England in 1807. Equiano's work details life in an Igbo village and his capture at age eleven, experiences as an enslaved person, self-emancipation, and his career as an abolitionist in England. Equiano is also the first person of African descent to serve in the British government and was a significant contributor to discussions that led to the formation of the West African nation of Sierra Leone.

"When I came to Kingston, I was surprised to see the number of Africans assembled together on Sundays; particularly at the large commodious place, called Spring Path. Here each different nation of Africa meet and dance after the manner of their own country. They still retain most of their native customs: they bury their dead, and put victuals, pipes, and tobacco, and other things in the grave with the corpse, in the same manner as in Africa."

Olaudah Equiano, Igbo abolitionist, author, and sailor

Kamala Harris (b. 1964) is an African American politician and lawyer. Harris is the highest-ranking woman in the history of the United States government, currently serving as the vice president to the 46th US president, Joe Biden. She is also the first person of African (more specifically, Jamaican) and South Asian descent to hold that position. Harris is part of the Democratic Party and served as a US senator, representing California, from 2017 to 2021. Prior to entering the second highest office in the US, she was the district attorney of San Francisco and attorney general of California. Harris famously spearheaded two major lawsuits that challenged the financial practices of major secondary institutions in the US. She is an alumna of Howard University, a leading HBCU (Historically Black College and University) located in Washington, DC.

"I think it's very important—as you have heard from so many incredible leaders—for us, at every moment in time, and certainly this one, to see the moment in time in which we exist and are present, and to be able to contextualize it, to understand where we exist in the history and in the moment as it relates not only to the past, but the future."

Kamala Harris, 49th vice president of the United States

EDUCATION AND KNOWLEDGE

Education lights the path to freedom. It is how we learn to navigate the world and make it bend to our will. Our elders and ancestors were often educated through a communal process. During enslavement, many ancestors learned to read and write in secret. There were entire secret schools located inside of homes where dozens of children would go to learn. Churches and community centers were also used in this capacity, and even today are often the first places where children learn about their history and culture. During liberation movements, elders and ancestors took it upon themselves to educate local community members of all ages, while providing other resources like food and housing.

Through education, we learn not just of the world but also about our positionality within it. To be educated is to gain understanding. However, it must be noted that education happens outside of the classroom as well. Learning cultural traditions like farming, cooking, building, sculpting, music, storytelling, and dance is an enriching experience. Whether within school systems or in other communal spaces, the best education comes from within the heart of the community and uses knowledge for the benefit of the whole.

The next sequence includes quotes that emphasize the necessity of education and the various forms of guidance, both formal and informal, that we receive within communities of the Pan African world.

artist | Erin K. Robinson, Untitled

Maurice Rupert Bishop (1944–1983) was the second prime minister of Grenada, an activist, a revolutionary, and leader of the New Jewel Movement (a revolutionary Marxist-Leninist vanguard party based in Grenada). He is best remembered for leading the overthrow of the Grenadian government in 1979 and becoming prime minister of Grenada until his assassination in 1983. Bishop was an influential advocate for Pan Africanism and the Non-Aligned Movement (NAM), as well as a supporter of progressive causes such as gender equality and workers' rights. He was described by some admirers as "the soul of Grenada." Bishop's legacy still resonates in his native land, where he is regarded to this day as a national hero. The Maurice Bishop International Airport was named in his honor.

"Education is *not* about certification. There are many certified fools in the world."

Maurice Rupert Bishop, former prime minister of Grenada

Na'im Akbar (b. 1944) is a clinical psychologist and Afrocentric educator. He is best known for his pioneering work in the field of Black psychology, an area of study that examines the psychological effects of racism on African Americans. As a student, Akbar was an activist in the Black Action Movement, a series of direct-action protests by Black students fighting against racism at the University of Michigan. He served as president of the Association of Black Psychologists from 1987 to 1988. He was a professor of psychology at Florida State University. Over the course of his career, he has written numerous books and journal articles and has given numerous lectures exploring how racial trauma can manifest within individuals and communities. His most notable book is *Know Thyself* (1999).

"When our young people know that there are no limits to their potential in the world of manufacturing, communication, physics, chemistry, or the science of the human mind, then those same young Black minds who create dances on the dance floor or compose music on their bodies with the 'hand jive' will recreate these fields of human endeavor with the same incomparability."

Na'im Akbar, African American and
Afrocentric clinical psychologist and author

Haile Selassie I (1892–1975) is one of the most influential figures in modern African history. Haile Selassie became emperor of Ethiopia in 1930, with his reign ending in 1974. He is credited with introducing sweeping reforms to Ethiopia's infrastructure, economy, and military, transforming it into an independent nation-state recognized on the world stage. He was also a staunch advocate of Pan Africanism, which sought to unify African nations and eliminate European colonial rule. Selassie was widely revered as a spiritual leader for the Rastafari movement, which holds him in high esteem as the returned messiah and living God. He died in 1975 at the age of eighty-three and his legacy lives on today, especially as a symbol of Rastafarian pride.

"Education and the quest for knowledge only stops at the grave."

Haile Selassie I, Ethiopian emperor from 1930 to 1974

ce Hall (ca. 1735–1807) was an African American abolitionist, st, and institution builder. He was the founder of the first lodge ack Freemasonry, African Lodge 1, established in 1784 in the ter several petitions from Hall and about a dozen other African ican men. Hall's dedication to social justice and the collective re of Black people is rooted in his sentiments toward slave society whole. Having escaped slavery, Hall remained a staunch opponent very and all aspects of the old colonial regime, advocating for ghts and access to education for African Americans and forming frican Society House. Hall was also involved in the repatriation ment, encouraging African Americans to return to Africa and e new lives within their motherland.

"Although you are deprived of the means of education; yet you are not deprived of the means of meditation; by which I mean thinking, hearing and weighing matters, men and things in your own mind, and making that judgment of them as you think reasonable to satisfy your minds and give an answer to those who may ask you a question. This nature hath furnished you with, without letter learning; and some have made great progress therein."

Prince Hall, father of Black Freemasonry, abolitionist, and activist

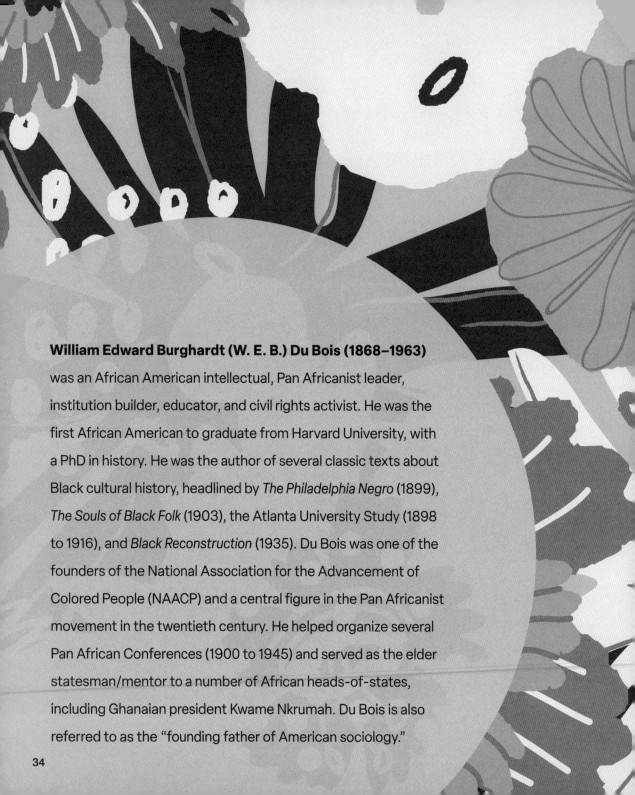

William Edward Burghardt (W. E. B.) Du Bois (1868–1963)
was an African American intellectual, Pan Africanist leader,
institution builder, educator, and civil rights activist. He was the
first African American to graduate from Harvard University, with
a PhD in history. He was the author of several classic texts about
Black cultural history, headlined by *The Philadelphia Negro* (1899),
The Souls of Black Folk (1903), the Atlanta University Study (1898
to 1916), and *Black Reconstruction* (1935). Du Bois was one of the
founders of the National Association for the Advancement of
Colored People (NAACP) and a central figure in the Pan Africanist
movement in the twentieth century. He helped organize several
Pan African Conferences (1900 to 1945) and served as the elder
statesman/mentor to a number of African heads-of-states,
including Ghanaian president Kwame Nkrumah. Du Bois is also
referred to as the "founding father of American sociology."

"THE FUNCTION OF THE UNIVERSITY IS NOT SIMPLY TO TEACH BREADWINNING, OR TO FURNISH TEACHERS FOR THE PUBLIC SCHOOLS, OR TO BE A CENTER OF POLITE SOCIETY; IT IS, ABOVE ALL, TO BE THE ORGAN OF THAT FINE ADJUSTMENT BETWEEN REAL LIFE AND THE GROWING KNOWLEDGE OF LIFE, AN ADJUSTMENT WHICH FORMS THE SECRET OF CIVILIZATION."

W. E. B. Du Bois, African American sociologist, Pan Africanist, author, and civil rights activist

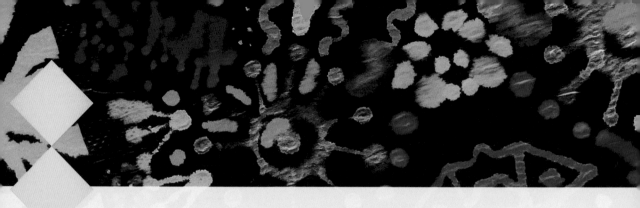

Mĩcere Gĩthae Mũgo (1942–2023) was a Kenyan playwright, poet, and activist. Born in Nyeri District, she is best known for her works that critique social inequalities and injustices within the African continent. Among her most celebrated plays is *The Trial of Dedan Kimathi* (1976), coauthored with fellow playwright Ngũgĩ wa Thiong'o, the renowned Kenyan author and novelist. Mũgo was awarded the Lifetime Achievement Award in African Literature from the African Royal Society in 2021. She is also known widely for her book of poetry, *My Mother's Poem and Other Songs* (1994). Due to her activism for justice and human rights, Mũgo was exiled from her home country of Kenya. Mũgo was a professor in the African American Studies department at Syracuse University and helped launch its Pan African Studies program in Syracuse, New York.

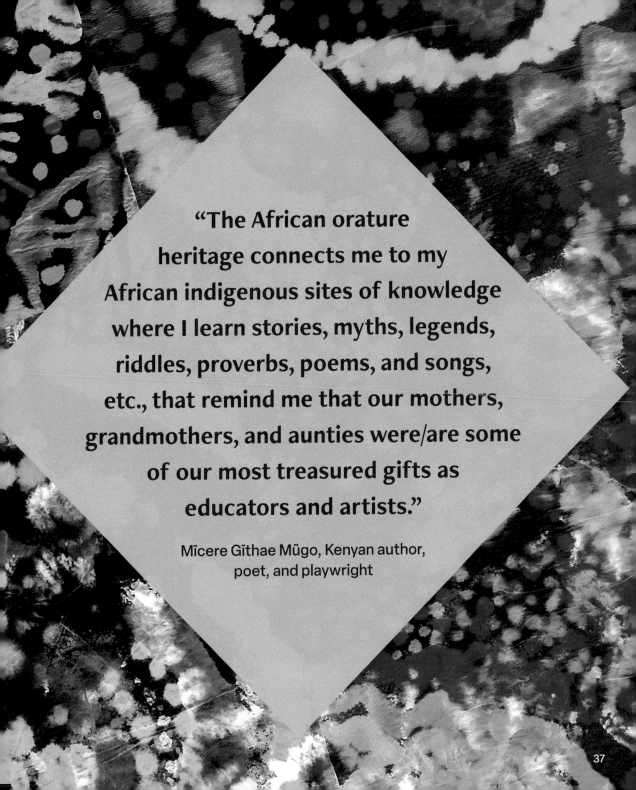

"The African orature heritage connects me to my African indigenous sites of knowledge where I learn stories, myths, legends, riddles, proverbs, poems, and songs, etc., that remind me that our mothers, grandmothers, and aunties were/are some of our most treasured gifts as educators and artists."

Mĩcere Gĩthae Mũgo, Kenyan author, poet, and playwright

Martha Euphemia Lofton Haynes (1890–1980) was an African American mathematician, educator, and trailblazer in the field of mathematics education. She was born in Washington, DC, graduated from Miner Teachers College in 1909, and earned her PhD at the Catholic University of America in 1943, becoming the first African American woman to earn a doctorate degree in mathematics. Throughout her career, Euphemia Haynes was dedicated to the advancement of mathematics education. She taught math for forty-seven years at various schools and institutions in Washington, DC, and was later appointed as chairperson of the Mathematics Department at Miner Teachers College, now known as the University of the District of Columbia. She also cofounded the Catholic Interracial Council of the District of Columbia.

"For a person of intelligence is well equipped to solve the problems of life . . . Let each defeat be a source of a new endeavor and each victory the strengthening of our spirit of gratitude and charity towards the unsuccessful."

Euphemia Haynes, African American mathematician and educator

JUSTICE, CIVIL RIGHTS, AND HUMAN RIGHTS

People of the Pan African world have long maintained a communal compass toward justice and restoration. Justice has always been a key issue of community concern, both internally and externally. Justice is the work enacted to right wrongs and ensure that pain, anguish, and trauma never happen again. It is the work toward ensuring that the civil and human rights of communities and individuals remain secure and protected. When seeking justice, we must implement steps to restore the harmed person or community—that is what it truly looks like. For centuries, Black communities throughout the Pan African world have demanded justice and asserted the right for self-determination. This includes the right to self-governance, seeking not just autonomy but also the ability to protect and restore the most vulnerable among us. A big part of this process has been truth telling. Every movement for civil rights, human rights, and justice has begun with a truth teller, lifting up their voice to speak truth to power. Oftentimes, this truth telling was met with hostility and pressure from oppressive systems and governments. Yet, they still spoke out of necessity, out of their calling.

In a world that often stigmatizes and sidelines Black communities, obtaining justice can be a difficult task. Thus, the road toward justice includes persistence, constant truth telling, and continual activism.

This next sequence highlights various perspectives on justice, including why it's needed, what it looks like, how it feels, and what happens when justice is fulfilled.

artist | Erin K. Robinson, *Note to Self*

Dr. Frantz Fanon (1925–1961) was a psychiatrist, philosopher, and revolutionary thinker from Martinique who wrote extensively on the psychological impact of colonialism and its legacy of racism. His most influential works include *Les damnés de la terre* (*The Wretched of the Earth*, 1961), *Peau noire, masques blancs* (*Black Skin, White Masks,* 1952), and *L'An V de la révolution algérienne* (*A Dying Colonialism*, 1959). Fanon's ideas had a major influence on anti-colonial and postcolonial thought, as well as on the emerging field of critical race theory. His writings continue to inspire people today who seek to challenge and upend oppressive systems of power. He is remembered for his passionate commitment to social justice and human liberation.

"EACH generation, in relative opacity, must DISCOVER its mission, FULFILL it, or otherwise betray it."

Frantz Fanon, Martinican psychiatrist

Ida B. Wells (1862–1931) was an African American journalist, activist, and leader in the civil rights movement of the late-nineteenth and early-twentieth centuries. Her tenacious fight against lynching and Jim Crow laws helped lay the groundwork for the modern civil rights movement. She investigated and documented lynchings in depth and published the pamphlets entitled *Southern Horrors: Lynch Law in All Its Phases* in 1892 and *The Red Record* in 1895, in addition to articles in Black-owned newspapers nationally. She was a cofounder of the National Association of Colored Women (NACW) and the NAACP. She was an indefatigable campaigner for justice who used her voice to bring attention to the injustices faced by African Americans.

"If this work can contribute in any way toward proving this, and at the same time arouse the conscience of the American people to a demand for justice to every citizen, and punishment by law for the lawless, I shall feel I have done my race a service."

Ida B. Wells, African American journalist and activist

Winnie Madikizela-Mandela (1936–2018) was a South African anti-apartheid activist and politician. She first rose to prominence as the wife of Nelson Mandela during his imprisonment from 1963 until his release in 1990. Following her husband's election as president of South Africa in 1994, Mandela became an outspoken advocate for women's rights and social justice. She was an active member of the African National Congress (ANC) Women's League, becoming one of South Africa's most visible symbols of resistance against apartheid. Mandela remained politically active until her death on April 2, 2018. Her legacy lives on in the struggle for human rights and social justice in South Africa.

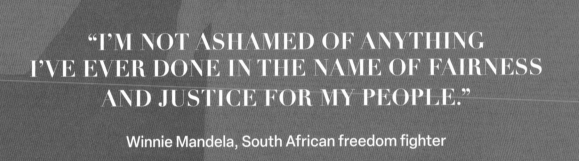

"I'M NOT ASHAMED OF ANYTHING
I'VE EVER DONE IN THE NAME OF FAIRNESS
AND JUSTICE FOR MY PEOPLE."

Winnie Mandela, South African freedom fighter

Harriet Tubman (ca. 1822–1913) was an African American abolitionist, activist, and soldier. Originally named Araminta Ross, she was born into slavery during the first quarter of the nineteenth century, but eventually escaped in 1849, finding asylum in Pennsylvania. Tubman is known as the greatest "conductor" of the Underground Railroad and the "Moses of her people," having liberated dozens of people from slavery, including her family members. One of her incredible achievements occurred in South Carolina during the American Civil War, in an event called the Combahee River Raid, when Tubman led Black Union soldiers into battle. She was the first woman to lead in this capacity during the Civil War. About 750 enslaved African Americans were freed as a result. After many years as a freedom fighter, Tubman engaged in the struggle for women's rights in Washington, DC.

"**There are two things I've got a right to, and these are, Death or Liberty—one or the other I mean to have. No one will take me back alive; I shall fight for my liberty, and when the time has come for me to go, the Lord will let them, kill me.**"

Harriet Tubman, African American liberator, abolitionist, and leader of the Underground Railroad

Mary Church Terrell (1863–1954) was an African American educator, orator, intellectual, and activist. She was one of the founding members of the National Association for the Advancement of Colored People, the Colored Women's League, the National Association of Colored Women, and the National Association of College Women. Terrell remained a staunch advocate for women's and civil rights throughout her life and vehemently protested discrimination of all forms in the US and Europe. She achieved a number of victories over her long career as an activist, including, but not restricted to, several challenges to the federal government that culminated with an antidiscrimination case against a private business owner in Washington, DC, when she was ninety years old. She published an autobiography in 1940 titled *A Colored Woman in a White World*.

"The chasm between the principles upon which this Government was founded, in which it still professes to believe, and those which are daily practiced under the protection of the flag, yawn so wide and deep."

Mary Church Terrell,
African American activist,
orator, and educator

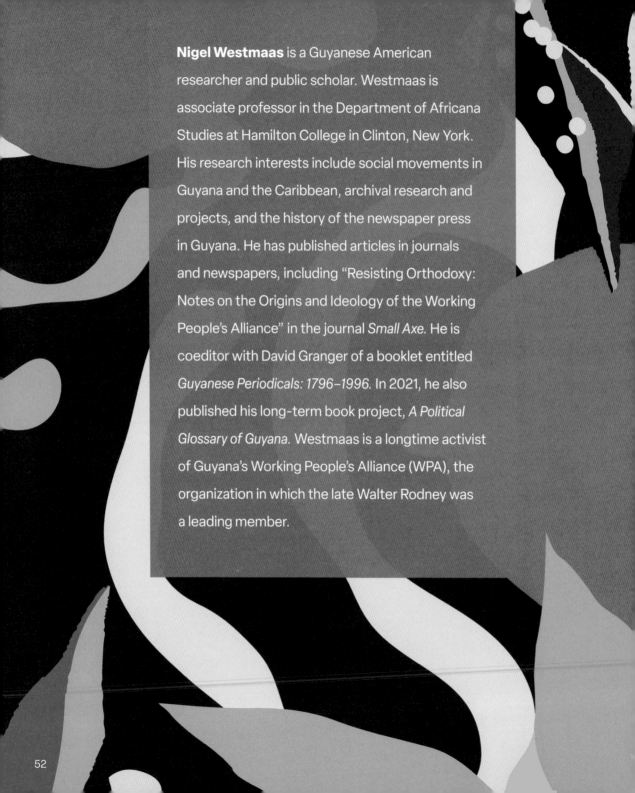

Nigel Westmaas is a Guyanese American researcher and public scholar. Westmaas is associate professor in the Department of Africana Studies at Hamilton College in Clinton, New York. His research interests include social movements in Guyana and the Caribbean, archival research and projects, and the history of the newspaper press in Guyana. He has published articles in journals and newspapers, including "Resisting Orthodoxy: Notes on the Origins and Ideology of the Working People's Alliance" in the journal *Small Axe.* He is coeditor with David Granger of a booklet entitled *Guyanese Periodicals: 1796–1996.* In 2021, he also published his long-term book project, *A Political Glossary of Guyana.* Westmaas is a longtime activist of Guyana's Working People's Alliance (WPA), the organization in which the late Walter Rodney was a leading member.

"THE ONLY THING MORE HORRIFYING THAN **INCIVILITY IN THE NATION** IS THE SHEER INDIFFERENCE AND COMPLACENCY OF FOLKS AROUND US. AND 'CIVILITY' IN A CERTAIN WAY IS PART OF THE **COMPLACENCY** OVER INJUSTICE AND MAY WELL BE DEPLOYED AS SUTURE TO OPPRESSION."

Nigel Westmaas, Guyanese American scholar and writer

RACE AND RACISM

Though race is a social construct, race and racism have very serious ramifications throughout society. The creation and elevation of race was weaponized against people of the Pan African world to justify enslavement and colonization. The concept was used to paint false narratives about entire groups of people based on biased perceptions and phenotype. Perpetrators of racism then tried to dehumanize people of African descent and other groups of people throughout the world who were of non-European ancestry. These attempts at subjugation based on race included enslavement, colonization, segregation, and apartheid (with varying harms within each system of oppression).

However, people of the Pan African world fought back and challenged racism along with the unjust systems operating on racist ideology. Black activists and scholars have critically deconstructed both race and racism, highlighted the nefarious ways by which race and racism have affected our lives, and used various strategies to empower their communities in the face of race-based discrimination.

Activists have also utilized the construct of race within liberation movements for the purpose of organizing and community activism. Examples of this include the Négritude movement of the 1930s among African and Caribbean writers and activists, the Black Power movement in the United States and Caribbean in the 1960s, and the Black Consciousness movement of South Africa, also during the 1960s. Blackness was used as a symbol of resistance. It became a political mantra for self-empowerment and strength.

This next sequence includes quotes that discuss the harms of racism and why it's necessary to counter racism at every level.

artist | Rendani Nemakhavhani, *Noema Magazine*

Rosie Perez (b. 1964) is a leading Afro–Puerto Rican actress, dancer, choreographer, director, and social activist. She rose to fame in the early 1990s with her memorable roles in films and TV shows such as *Do the Right Thing* (1989), *White Men Can't Jump* (1992), *In Living Color* (1990–1994), and *Fearless* (1993). She has received multiple Emmy nominations for her roles in *The Flight Attendant* (2020–present) and *In Living Color*. In addition to her acting career, she is a dedicated advocate for the rights of women and people of color. Perez truly embodies what it means to be a multifaceted artist, paving the way for generations to come.

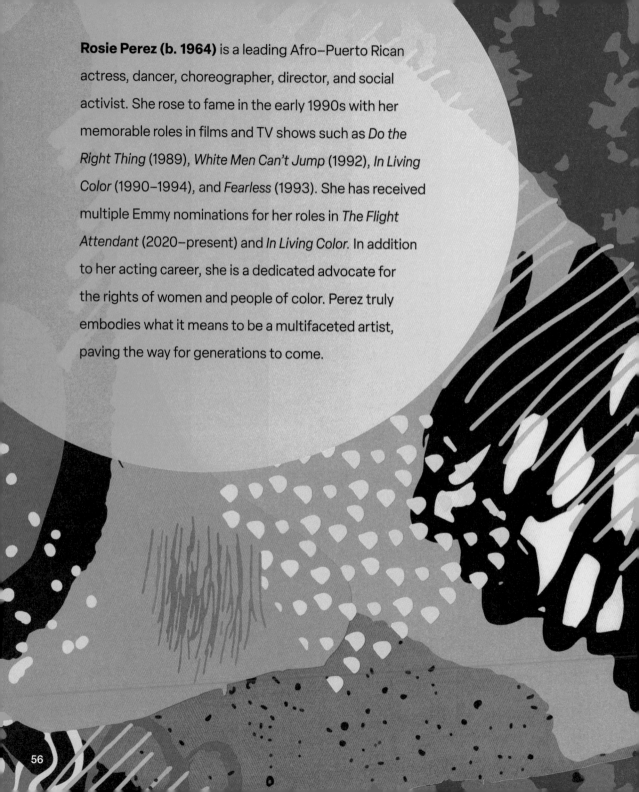

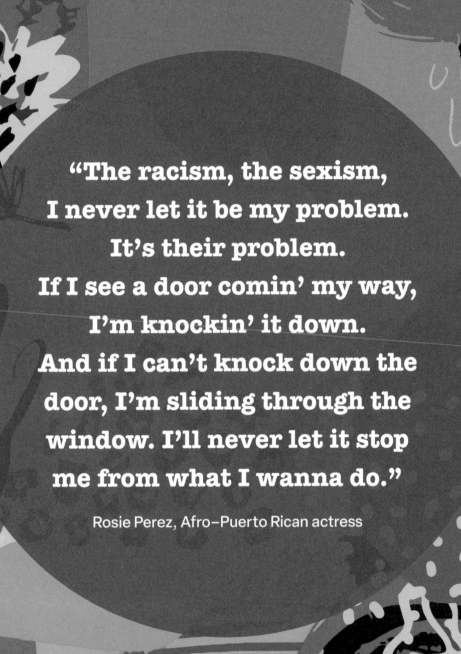

"The racism, the sexism,
I never let it be my problem.
It's their problem.
If I see a door comin' my way,
I'm knockin' it down.
And if I can't knock down the
door, I'm sliding through the
window. I'll never let it stop
me from what I wanna do."

Rosie Perez, Afro–Puerto Rican actress

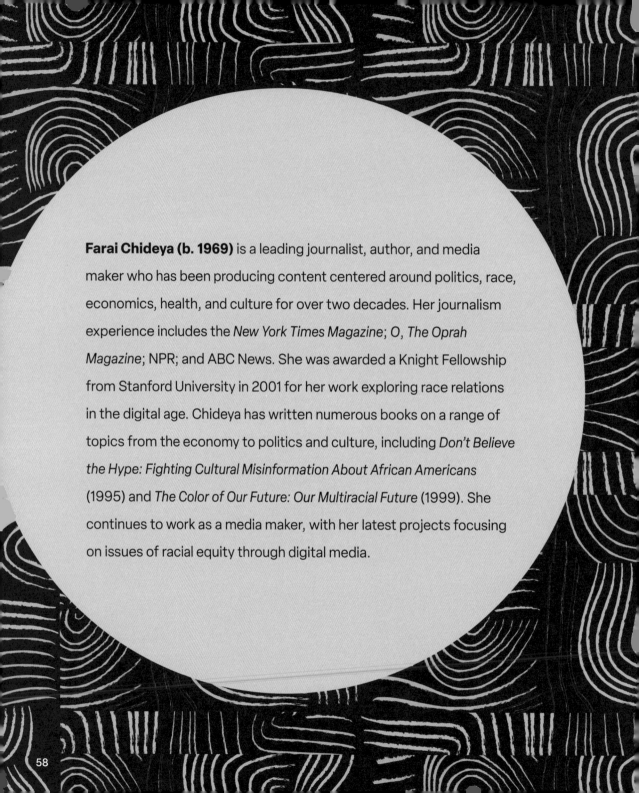

Farai Chideya (b. 1969) is a leading journalist, author, and media maker who has been producing content centered around politics, race, economics, health, and culture for over two decades. Her journalism experience includes the *New York Times Magazine*; *O, The Oprah Magazine*; NPR; and ABC News. She was awarded a Knight Fellowship from Stanford University in 2001 for her work exploring race relations in the digital age. Chideya has written numerous books on a range of topics from the economy to politics and culture, including *Don't Believe the Hype: Fighting Cultural Misinformation About African Americans* (1995) and *The Color of Our Future: Our Multiracial Future* (1999). She continues to work as a media maker, with her latest projects focusing on issues of racial equity through digital media.

"The first step in resolving some of the tension between the races in this country is to talk about these issues honestly. Racism unexamined will always be racism unresolved."

Farai Chideya, African American journalist

Benjamin Banneker (1731–1806) was a mathematician, astronomer, land surveyor, scientist, engineer, and abolitionist. He was "born free" in Ellicott Mills, Maryland, to free parents. Banneker built the first operating clock in America and also initiated a string of correspondence with Thomas Jefferson, advocating for the freedom of enslaved Africans. Additionally, Banneker used his expertise in astronomy to author a series of almanacs, providing weather predictions and other astronomical forecasts. Some biographers believe that Banneker was a descendant of the Dogon people of West Africa, known for their expertise in astronomy. Perhaps his most famous feat was a contribution to the surveying of Washington, DC.

"Sir, I freely and Cheerfully acknowledge, that I am of the African race, and in that colour which is natural to them of the deepest dye, and it is under a Sense of the most profound gratitude to the Supreme Ruler of the universe, that I now confess to you, that I am not under that State of tyrannical thraldom, and inhuman captivity, to which too many of my brethren are doomed; but that I have abundantly tasted of the fruition of those blessings which proceed from that free and unequalled liberty with which you are favoured and which I hope you will willingly allow you have received from the immediate hand of that Being, from whom proceedeth every good and perfect gift."

Benjamin Banneker, African American mathematician, astronomer, and abolitionist

Paul Stephenson (b. 1937) is a Black British civil rights activist, campaigner, and public speaker who was awarded the status of Officer of the Most Excellent Order of the British Empire (OBE) in 2009 for his work in race equality. He has championed the cause of racial justice since the 1960s, first becoming involved with the anti-racist Bristol Bus Boycott. He is credited with helping to desegregate Britain. He became famous after being denied service at the Bay Horse pub in Bristol, UK, and refusing to leave. Since then, he has been involved in a number of civil rights campaigns. He is a regular contributor to national newspapers and frequently appears on radio and television programs to discuss issues of race equality.

"You can't have true racial harmony without racial justice. So, you need to be disruptive."

Paul Stephenson, Black British
civil rights activist of
West African descent

Dr. Kimani Nehusi currently teaches at the Department of Africology and African American Studies at Temple University. His scholarship is distinguished by strong interests in the holistic study of the Afrikan World, from ancient times to the future, and of the Caribbean and Guyana. His perspective is an Afrocological one in which Afrikan phenomena are simultaneously accessible from approaches that are usually termed language and linguistics, history, and culture, utilizing a robust research methodology. Nehusi attended St. Bartholomew's Anglican School in his village of Queenstown, on the Essequibo Coast in Guyana, and holds a BA and an MA from the University of Guyana and a PhD from University College London. Furthermore, he holds a Diploma in Egyptology from the University of London, where he also undertook advanced studies in Egyptology, including advanced translation of Middle and Late Egyptian texts.

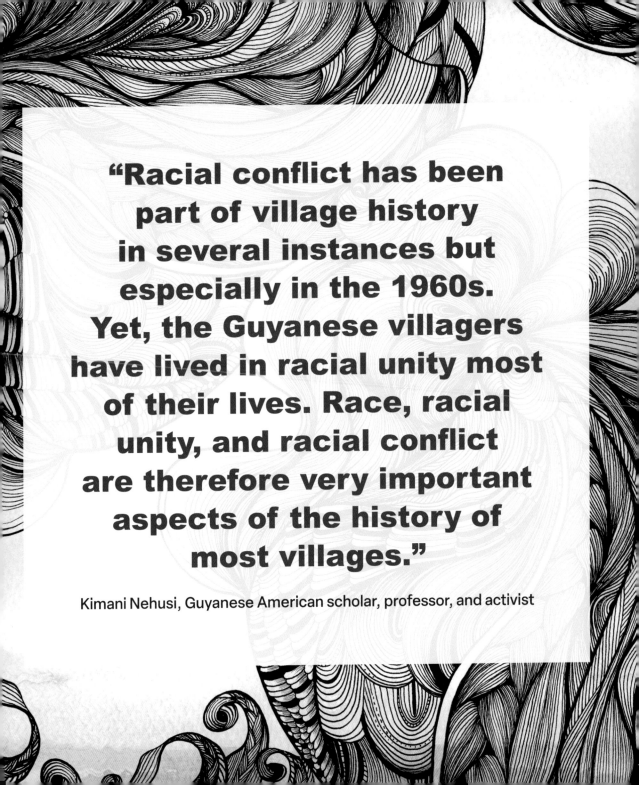

"Racial conflict has been part of village history in several instances but especially in the 1960s. Yet, the Guyanese villagers have lived in racial unity most of their lives. Race, racial unity, and racial conflict are therefore very important aspects of the history of most villages."

Kimani Nehusi, Guyanese American scholar, professor, and activist

Festus Claudius McKay (1890–1948), better known as Claude McKay, was a Jamaican American writer, poet, and literary critic. He is most often credited with initiating the Harlem Renaissance with the classic lamentation, "If We Must Die." At the close of World War I, he visited Europe, which had a profound effect on his later life. Upon his return he became a communist and imposed the race question into political discourse. Throughout his career, McKay wrote short stories, novels, and multiple volumes of poetry. His most popular novellas are *Home to Harlem* (1928) and *Banjo* (1929), while *Harlem Shadows* (1922) remains his most prominent volume of poetry.

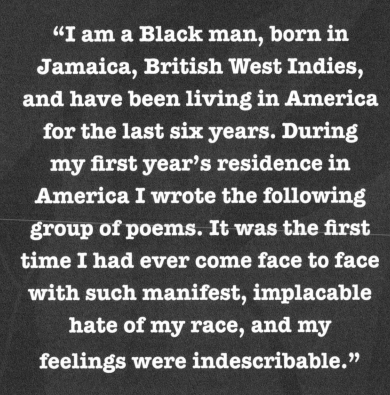

"I am a Black man, born in Jamaica, British West Indies, and have been living in America for the last six years. During my first year's residence in America I wrote the following group of poems. It was the first time I had ever come face to face with such manifest, implacable hate of my race, and my feelings were indescribable."

Claude McKay, Jamaican American poet, writer, and Harlem Renaissance figure

Robert Smalls (1839–1915) was a political leader during and after Reconstruction in South Carolina. Born a slave in Beaufort, South Carolina, he became a politician and, later, a businessman as a freedman. During the American Civil War he became notable for his daring escape from slavery from Confederate-controlled territory in a Confederate transport ship, which he then sailed to the Union blockade. As a result, Smalls became an American hero and was perceived as a symbol of freedom during Reconstruction. After emancipation, Smalls joined the Republican Party and quickly rose to prominence in the South Carolina state legislature. In 1868, he was elected to the United States House of Representatives, where he served five terms during Reconstruction.

"My race needs no special defense,
for the past history of them in this country
proves them to be equal of any people
anywhere. All they need is an equal chance
in the battle of life."

Robert Smalls, African American politician and former United States
representative for the state of South Carolina

GENDER, FEMINISM, AND WOMANISM

Throughout the course of history, women of the Pan African world have demonstrated power, tenacity, and intellect. They have participated in and led major movements for freedom and liberation. Across the continent of Africa and throughout the diaspora, Black women played a central role in elevating our communities as thought leaders, innovators, and changemakers. From Beatriz Kimpa Vita (the Mother of Black Liberation) to Harriet Tubman (our Moses), women of the Pan African world have always lived purposeful lives filled with conviction, hope, and inspiration. Worldwide, the lives of women and girls are often suppressed, and they endure the toughest of hardships.

Due to systemic oppression, racism, and sexism, Black women and girls are often vulnerable, in need of additional care and resources. Black women authors, activists, storytellers, freedom seekers, and truth tellers have repeatedly taken the reins toward implementing a more just, free, and equitable world. Black women and girls are often placed in the position of changemaker out of both tenacity and necessity. From the origins of humanity to the rising sisterhood of today, women of the Pan African world have given us thousands of years' worth of insightful experiences and triumphs to guide our paths toward a greater future.

The following sequence of quotes features women and men from the African continent and throughout the diaspora expressing the importance of supporting and elevating women and girls within our communities.

artist | Erin K. Robinson, *Aquarius*

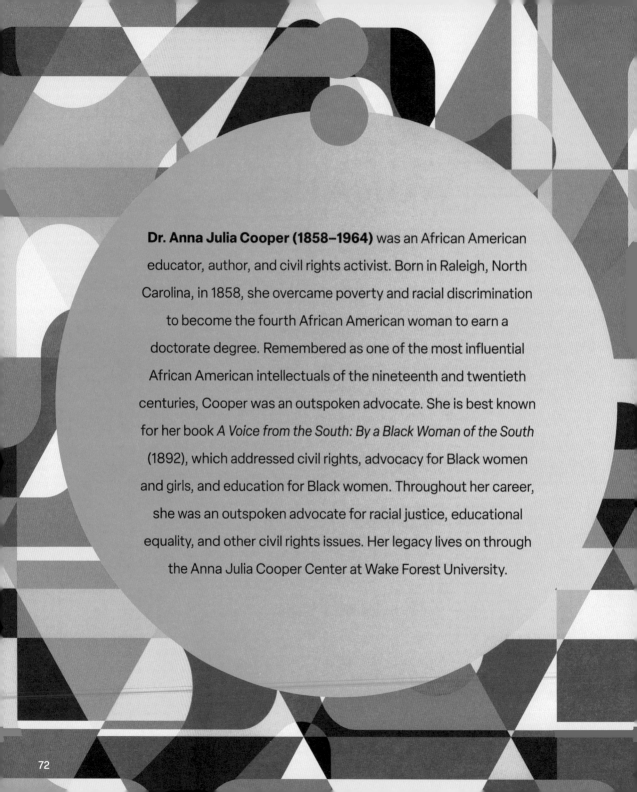

Dr. Anna Julia Cooper (1858–1964) was an African American educator, author, and civil rights activist. Born in Raleigh, North Carolina, in 1858, she overcame poverty and racial discrimination to become the fourth African American woman to earn a doctorate degree. Remembered as one of the most influential African American intellectuals of the nineteenth and twentieth centuries, Cooper was an outspoken advocate. She is best known for her book *A Voice from the South: By a Black Woman of the South* (1892), which addressed civil rights, advocacy for Black women and girls, and education for Black women. Throughout her career, she was an outspoken advocate for racial justice, educational equality, and other civil rights issues. Her legacy lives on through the Anna Julia Cooper Center at Wake Forest University.

"The position of woman in society determines the vital elements of its regeneration and progress."

Anna Julia Cooper, African American
educator and activist

The Combahee River Collective (1974–1980) was an organization of Black feminists and lesbians founded in 1974. The organization worked to empower Black women through revolutionary action, activism, and critical dialogue. Through their organizing, the Collective sought to challenge racism and sexism as well as homophobia and classism within struggles for liberation. By recognizing that all forms of oppression are interconnected, the Collective developed an intersectional approach to activism and advocacy that continues to inform current social justice movements in the United States. Additionally, they pushed for the development of Black feminist theory and praxis, which is still used today as a tool for dismantling oppression. The Collective disbanded in 1980, but its legacy lives on.

"There have always been Black women activists—some known, like Sojourner Truth, Harriet Tubman, Frances E. W. Harper, Ida B. Wells Barnett, and Mary Church Terrell, and thousands upon thousands unknown—who have had a shared awareness of how their sexual identity combined with their racial identity to make their whole life situation and the focus of their political struggles unique. Contemporary Black feminism is the outgrowth of countless generations of personal sacrifice, militancy, and work by our mothers and sisters."

The Combahee River Collective,
organization of Black feminists and lesbians

Queen Yaa Asantewaa (1840–1921) was the Queen Mother of the Ejisu people within the Ashanti Empire, in modern-day Ghana. She became a prominent figure in West African history when she led her people in battle against British colonialism in 1900, during what has become known as the War of the Golden Stool. The Golden Stool represented the soul of the Ashanti people; thus Asantewaa rallied troops to protect it and the sovereignty of her people. Some Ashanti warriors hesitated to defend the stool. Queen Asantewaa's persistence inspired her people to fight. As a result, the British were never able to get access to the stool. However, Asantewaa was exiled to Seychelles, where she later died. She was known for her courage, strength, and leadership skills, which she used to protect her people from foreign forces. Queen Yaa Asantewaa was an inspiration for women in the region and has become a symbol of resistance against colonialism throughout West Africa.

"Is it true that the bravery of the Ashanti is no more? I cannot believe it. It cannot be! I must say this: If you the men of Ashanti will not go forward, then we will. We the women will. I shall call upon my fellow women."

Queen Yaa Asantewaa, Queen Mother of the Ejisu people

Justice Ketanji Brown Jackson (b. 1970) is an associate justice of the Supreme Court of the United States. She was appointed to the court by President Joe Biden in April 2021, and previously served as a judge on the United States District Court for the District of Columbia from 2013 to 2021. Prior to that, she was vice chair of the United States Sentencing Commission from 2010 to 2013. Justice Jackson was born in Washington, DC. She graduated magna cum laude from Harvard College in 1992 and obtained her law degree from Harvard Law School in 1996. Prior to joining the bench, Justice Jackson clerked for Judge Patti Saris on the United States District Court for Massachusetts, and then for Justice Stephen Breyer on the Supreme Court. She officially joined the United States Supreme Court in June 2022.

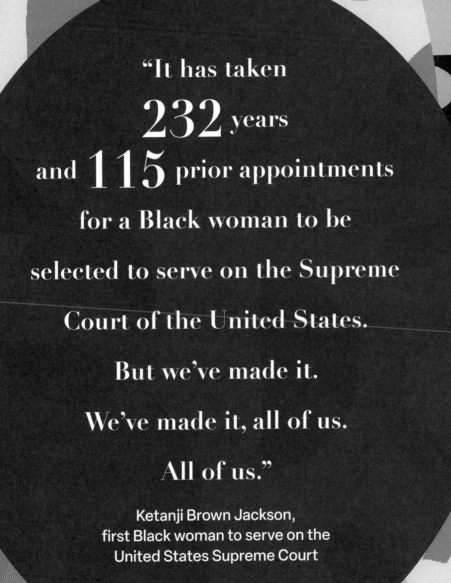

"It has taken

232 years

and **115** prior appointments

for a Black woman to be

selected to serve on the Supreme

Court of the United States.

But we've made it.

We've made it, all of us.

All of us."

Ketanji Brown Jackson,
first Black woman to serve on the
United States Supreme Court

Shirley Chisholm (1924–2005) was an African American politician, educator, and author. She was the first Black woman elected to Congress in 1968 and the first major-party Black candidate for president of the United States in 1972. Chisholm was the daughter of parents with Bajan and Guyanese roots. In 2015, she was posthumously awarded the Presidential Medal of Freedom. A leader in the civil rights movement and a founding member of the National Women's Political Caucus, Chisholm fought for gender and racial equality until her death in 2005. She was devoted to breaking barriers and worked tirelessly to raise awareness of issues affecting African Americans, women, and marginalized communities.

"Discrimination against women, solely on the basis of their sex, is so widespread that it seems to many persons normal, natural, and right. The time is clearly now to put this House on record for the fullest expression of that equality of opportunity which our founding fathers professed. They professed it, but they did not assure it to their daughters, as they tried to do for their sons. The Constitution they wrote was designed to protect the rights of white, male citizens. As there were no Black Founding Fathers, there were no founding mothers—a great pity, on both counts. It is not too late to complete the work they left undone. Today, here, we should start to do so."

Shirley Chisholm, first Black woman elected to the
United States Congress

Dwayne Wong (Omowale) (b. 1991) is a Guyanese-born author based in the United States who has written several books on the history and experiences of the African people, both on the continent of Africa and throughout the diaspora. His book, *Kingdoms and Civilizations of Africa* (2015), provides a primer on inspiring African kingdoms, including Songhai, Mali, Kanem-Borno, and more. Additionally, Wong uses social media to educate and engage audiences across a number of platforms. Using his wide reach, Wong teaches about African history and Pan Africanism to both inform and unite people of African descent across the diaspora.

"African women have always played a central role in the struggle against oppression. Nzinga is well-known in African history as the warrior queen who fought against the slave trade. On the other side of the Atlantic we find women such as Harriet Tubman in the United States and Nanny of the Maroons in Jamaica, both of whom fought against slavery. Funmilayo Ransome Kuti, Fela Kuti's mother, was a very prominent activist from Nigeria and she played an important role in Africa's struggle for independence from colonial rule. Rosa Parks, Yaa Asantewaa, Ida B. Wells-Barnett, and Dandara of Palmares are some more of the many examples of African women struggling against the oppression of their people."

Dwayne Wong (Omowale), Guyanese American author and Pan African activist

Madam C. J. Walker (1867–1919) was an African American businesswoman, social justice advocate, and philanthropist. She was born Sarah Breedlove in 1867 to former enslaved African Americans. Through entrepreneurship in the Black hair care industry, she became one of the wealthiest self-made female entrepreneurs and the first Black woman millionaire in the United States. In 1910, Madam Walker launched the Madam C. J. Walker Manufacturing Company, which sold her very own brand of hair and beauty products for African American women. Her success was so great that she opened factories in Pittsburgh and Indianapolis to help meet the demand for her products. By 1912, Walker had established herself as a powerful leader in the African American community, a mentor to Black entrepreneurs, and a generous philanthropist seeking to improve the lives of African Americans.

"I am not merely satisfied in making money for myself. I am endeavoring to provide employment for hundreds of women of my race."

Madam C. J. Walker, first Black woman millionaire in the United States

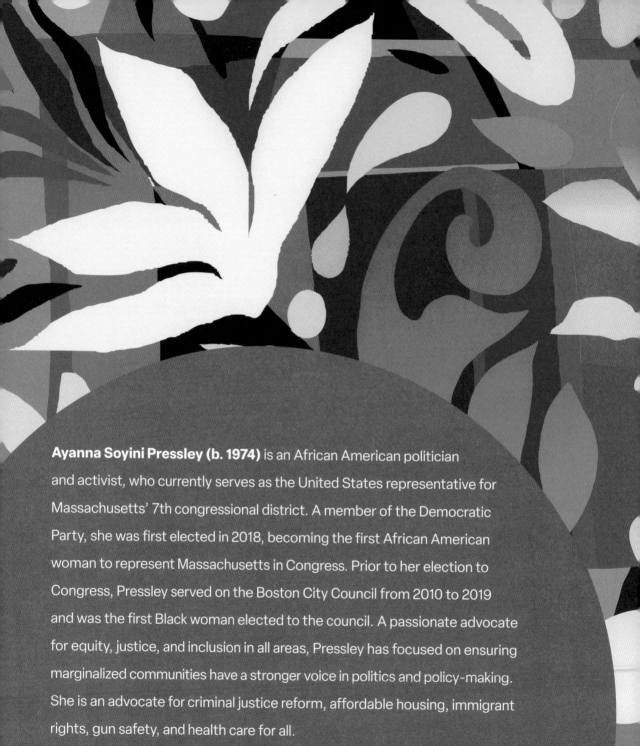

Ayanna Soyini Pressley (b. 1974) is an African American politician and activist, who currently serves as the United States representative for Massachusetts' 7th congressional district. A member of the Democratic Party, she was first elected in 2018, becoming the first African American woman to represent Massachusetts in Congress. Prior to her election to Congress, Pressley served on the Boston City Council from 2010 to 2019 and was the first Black woman elected to the council. A passionate advocate for equity, justice, and inclusion in all areas, Pressley has focused on ensuring marginalized communities have a stronger voice in politics and policy-making. She is an advocate for criminal justice reform, affordable housing, immigrant rights, gun safety, and health care for all.

"FOR TOO LONG, BLACK GIRLS HAVE BEEN DISCRIMINATED AGAINST AND CRIMINALIZED FOR THE HAIR THAT GROWS ON OUR HEADS AND THE WAY WE MOVE THROUGH AND SHOW UP IN THIS WORLD. IN MY HOME STATE, THE COMMONWEALTH OF MASSACHUSETTS, TWO TWIN SISTERS, DEANNA AND MAYA, HIGH SCHOOL STUDENTS, WERE DISCIPLINED FOR SHOWING UP WITH BRAIDS. THEY WERE GIVEN NUMEROUS DETENTIONS, KICKED OFF THE TRACK TEAM, BANNED FROM PROM, SOLELY FOR THEIR HAIRSTYLE. IN THEIR OWN WORDS, THESE SCHOLARS AND ATHLETES WERE JUDGED MORE FOR THEIR HERITAGE THAN THEIR HOMEWORK. NO MORE."

Ayanna Pressley, African American politician and United States representative for the state of Massachusetts

PEACE AND LOVE

Love is how the soul heals and flourishes. It provides warmth and nourishment beyond our material needs. Communities of the Pan African world express love in various ways and it thrives within our life-sustaining traditions. Self-love and communal love are the basis of our movements for liberation because they empower the spirit to move in the face of fear. It can be a form of salvation, a way to protect and bind. It is where we gain the courage and the confidence to move forward with the reassurance of support. Every aspect of our lives draws upon love as a mechanism for strength, growth, understanding, and power.

It is even ingrained in our culinary traditions, by using food to comfort and cure. Love is ingrained in how we embrace our communities, using neighborhoods and close proximity to showcase communal pride and connections. Most of all, it is central to how we recognize and embrace our families, using family structures that are based on bonds that go far beyond the nuclear family. For example, cousins are more like brothers and sisters. "Friends of the family" are more like aunts and uncles. Aunts, uncles, and grandparents are like having another set of parents. Our families are expansive, historically utilized to meet our various needs. The familial bond expands to the community bond, which expands to a connection with the rest of humanity. The South African concept of Ubuntu ("I am because you are") embodies this. Its usefulness for embracing the humanity of others has been used in truth and reconciliation initiatives, as well as in the field of social work.

This centering of humanity. This centering of community and wholeness. This is reparative. This is healing. This is love.

The next sequence includes quotes about love and how it manifests in our daily lives through activism, self-care, and communal gatherings.

artist | Uzo Njoku, *The Flower Man*

bell hooks (1952–2021) was a renowned African American author, feminist, and social activist. Born Gloria Jean Watkins, she adopted the pseudonym bell hooks as an adult to honor her maternal great-grandmother. Throughout her career, hooks published over thirty books spanning topics such as gender, race, class, and oppression. She has become a source of inspiration and guidance to many, offering progressive solutions to social and cultural issues. She taught at The New School as a professor in residence. Her pioneering book, *Feminist Theory: From Margin to Center* (1984), is considered a staple in Black feminist teachings. hooks was an influential figure whose work seeks to inspire positive change for those suffering from oppression.

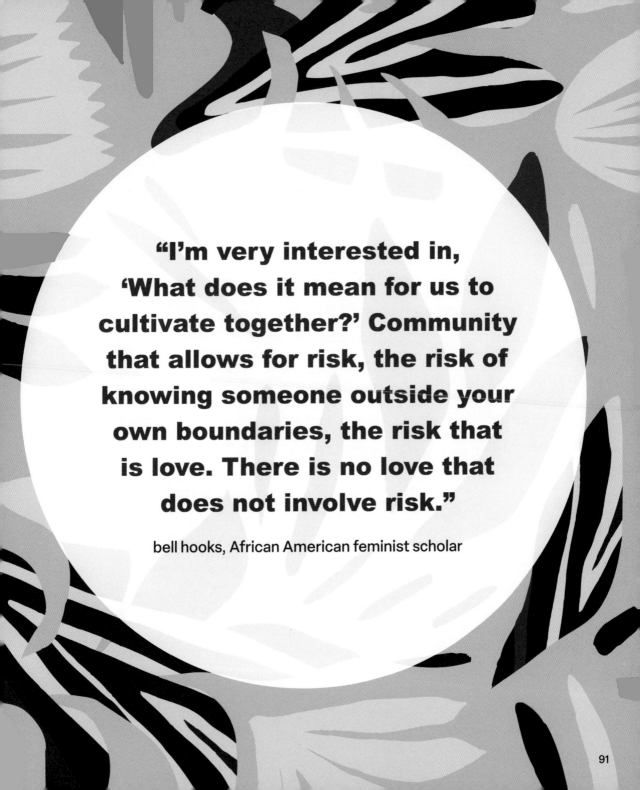

"I'm very interested in, 'What does it mean for us to cultivate together?' Community that allows for risk, the risk of knowing someone outside your own boundaries, the risk that is love. There is no love that does not involve risk."

bell hooks, African American feminist scholar

Basetsana Kumalo (b. 1974) is a South African television personality, entrepreneur, and philanthropist. She rose to prominence after winning Miss Soweto in 1990 and Miss South Africa in 1994 and has since gone on to become one of the most prominent figures in South African media. Outside of her TV career, she has also founded several successful businesses and is passionately involved with numerous charity initiatives. She is a powerful advocate for the empowerment of women and children in South Africa, and her impact can be felt across many different sectors of society as a Black woman business leader. Kumalo is an inspiring example of how dedication and hard work can lead to great success.

"Not everybody can be famous
but everybody can be great, because
greatness is determined by service . . .
You only need a heart full of grace
and a soul generated by love."

Basetsana Kumalo, South African businesswoman
and television personality

Thomas Sankara (1949–1987) was an iconic figure in West African history, remembered for his work as the former president of Burkina Faso from 1983 to 1987. He was a committed socialist and Pan Africanist who sought to improve the lives of the Burkinabé people through progressive social reform, anti-imperialist policy, and environmental sustainability. His policies and advocacy on behalf of the nation's most vulnerable citizens endeared him to many, making his tragically early death at the hands of a military coup in 1987 all the more painful. He is remembered as one of Africa's modern heroes, who remains an inspiration to those striving for social justice and economic progress throughout the continent.

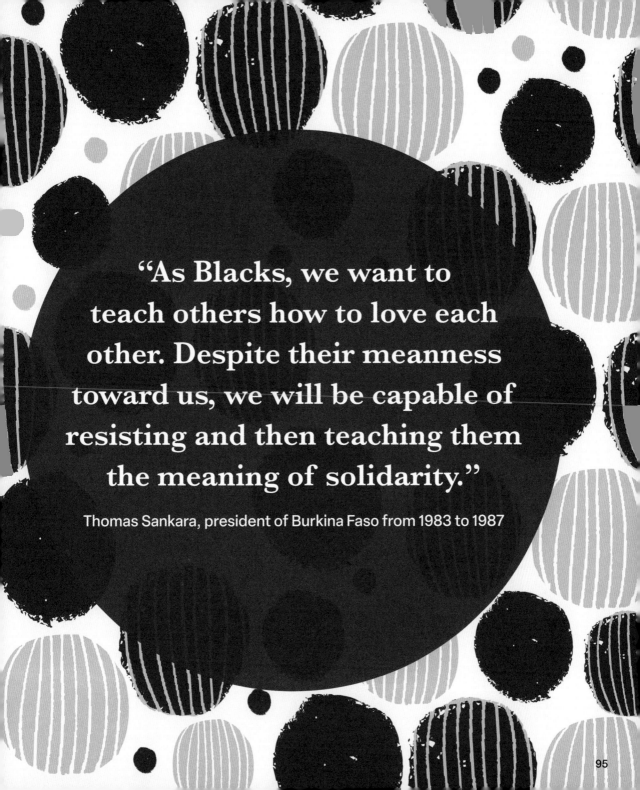

"As Blacks, we want to teach others how to love each other. Despite their meanness toward us, we will be capable of resisting and then teaching them the meaning of solidarity."

Thomas Sankara, president of Burkina Faso from 1983 to 1987

Phillis Wheatley (1753–1784) is widely recognized as the first African American poet to be published in the United States. Born in West Africa, she was kidnapped around the age of seven years old and sold into slavery. She became part of a family in New England who encouraged her education and soon discovered her talent as a writer. The family brought her to London, England, in 1773 and helped publish her book of poetry. After returning from London, Wheatley continued to write and published two books before her death in December 1784. Her works celebrated African American culture and faith, often referencing classical Greek and Roman mythology while addressing issues like slavery. She was an inspiration for future artists of color during the abolition movement and her works have been widely anthologized. Her legacy continues to inspire writers today.

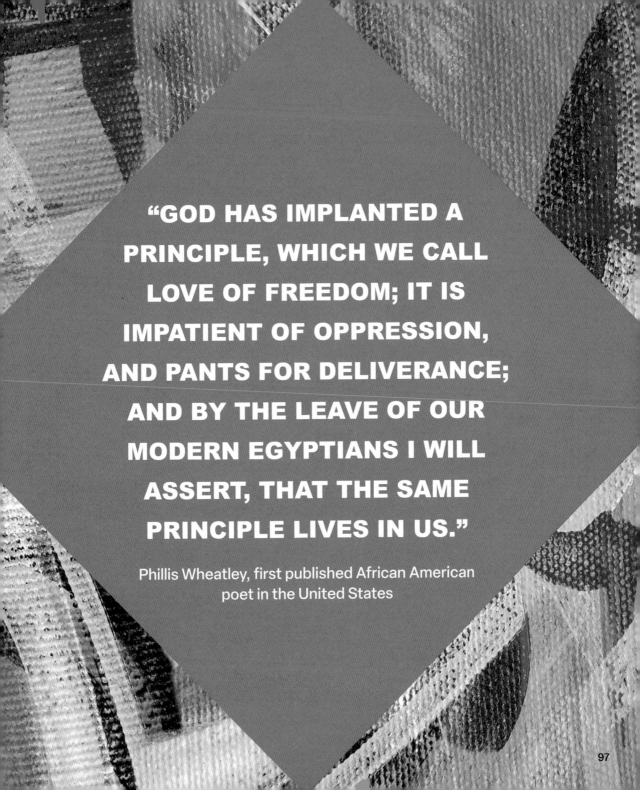

"GOD HAS IMPLANTED A PRINCIPLE, WHICH WE CALL LOVE OF FREEDOM; IT IS IMPATIENT OF OPPRESSION, AND PANTS FOR DELIVERANCE; AND BY THE LEAVE OF OUR MODERN EGYPTIANS I WILL ASSERT, THAT THE SAME PRINCIPLE LIVES IN US."

Phillis Wheatley, first published African American poet in the United States

Harper Glenn (b. 1980) is an African American writer of fiction. In addition to creating works rooted in underrepresented spaces, they are passionate about books that unveil the psychological, sociological, and economic disparities in poverty-stricken regions of the world. Born and raised in Georgia, Glenn now resides in Washington. Glenn's young adult speculative novel, *Monarch Rising*, was published in 2022. *Monarch Rising* is a dystopian, futuristic novel set in "New Georgia" that grapples with the balance between social order, the human condition, poverty, and love.

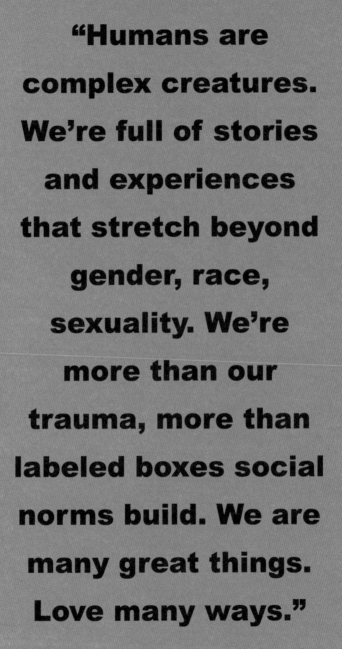

"Humans are complex creatures. We're full of stories and experiences that stretch beyond gender, race, sexuality. We're more than our trauma, more than labeled boxes social norms build. We are many great things. Love many ways."

Harper Glenn, African American fiction writer

William H. A. Moore (also known as W. H. A. Moore) was an African American poet and journalist during the New Negro Movement and Harlem Renaissance. In a 1904 essay published by the African Methodist Episcopal Church, Moore is cited describing the New Negro Literary Movement as "the culminating expression of a heart growth the most strange and attractive in American life." Moore published many of his poems in the *New York Age*, an African American newspaper that operated from 1887 to 1953. He is best known for his collection of poems, "Dusk Songs," which was published in James Weldon Johnson's *The Book of American Negro Poetry* in 1922 along with other rising and famed Black poets of the time.

"When the Dawn comes—

Dawn, deathless, dreaming—

I shall will that my soul must be cleansed of hate,

I shall pray for strength

to hold children close to my heart,

I shall desire

to build houses where the poor will know

shelter, comfort, beauty.

And then may I look

into a woman's eyes

And find holiness, love, and the peace

which passeth understanding."

William H. A. Moore, African American
poet of the Harlem Renaissance

David Walker (1785 or 1796–1830)
was a prominent African American abolitionist and author. Born free in Wilmington, North Carolina, he moved to Boston as a young man and opened a clothing store. He soon became an influential voice in the abolitionist movement, publishing his most famous work, *David Walker's Appeal*, in 1829. The *Appeal* was an impassioned plea for African Americans to fight for freedom and equality, and it had a profound influence on the course of the abolitionist struggle. Walker worked as a Boston writer and agent for *Freedom's Journal*, the first African American–owned newspaper in America. He spent his life actively advocating for the rights of African Americans and was a key figure in the fight for emancipation.

"Those philanthropists and lovers of the human family, who have volunteered their services for our redemption from wretchedness, have a high claim on our gratitude, and we should always view them as our greatest earthly benefactors."

David Walker, African American abolitionist and writer

INSPIRATION, HOPE, AND PERSEVERANCE

Inspiration is often the key to moving forward and unlocking the next step to success. Communities within the Pan African world are inspired by the achievements of key historical figures who have managed to conquer their fears and fulfill their destinies. For example, the great Toussaint Louverture led Haiti to its freedom from France, becoming the first free Black republic in the Western Hemisphere. Haiti's independence signaled the ability for transformative change to exist even during the harshest moments. It inspired enslaved and freed Africans across the Americas as a source of hope and reassurance that liberation is possible.

We are also inspired by those around us who are currently breaking new ground. With inspiration comes hope, with hope comes motivation, and with motivation comes action. The actions we take when inspired can lead to innovation, upward mobility, new freedom, and, most importantly, the personal satisfaction and confidence to keep going.

Inspiration is the precursor to movement and change. When inspired by our history and truths, we move forward within our communities, regions, and nations with the hope of building a better society and world that benefits us all. Future generations within the Pan African world rely on the stories of our collective persistence and perseverance as a guide for how far they can go standing on the shoulders of their ancestors.

The next sequence includes quotes from Black historical figures and contemporary persons who inspire us to reach new heights and encourage us on our quest to make the unbelievable achievable.

artist | Nicole Collie, *Father and Sons*

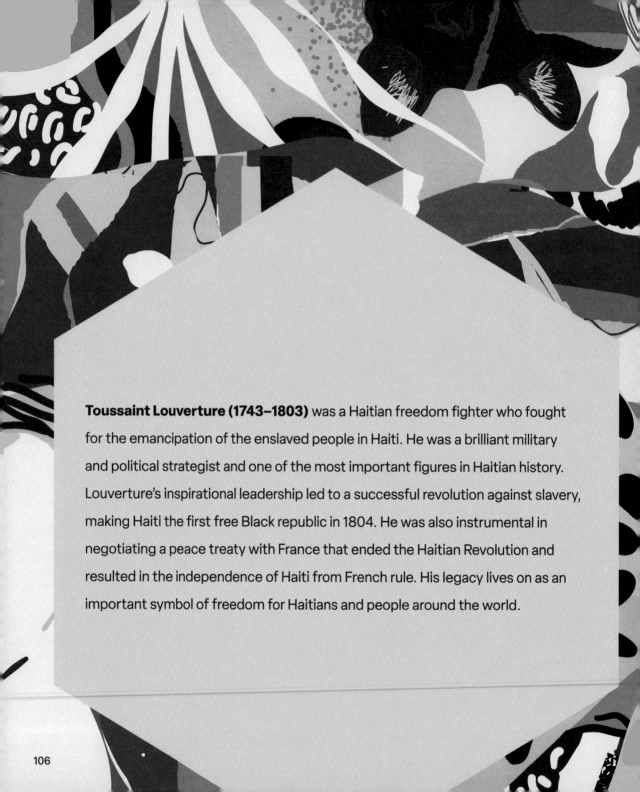

Toussaint Louverture (1743–1803) was a Haitian freedom fighter who fought for the emancipation of the enslaved people in Haiti. He was a brilliant military and political strategist and one of the most important figures in Haitian history. Louverture's inspirational leadership led to a successful revolution against slavery, making Haiti the first free Black republic in 1804. He was also instrumental in negotiating a peace treaty with France that ended the Haitian Revolution and resulted in the independence of Haiti from French rule. His legacy lives on as an important symbol of freedom for Haitians and people around the world.

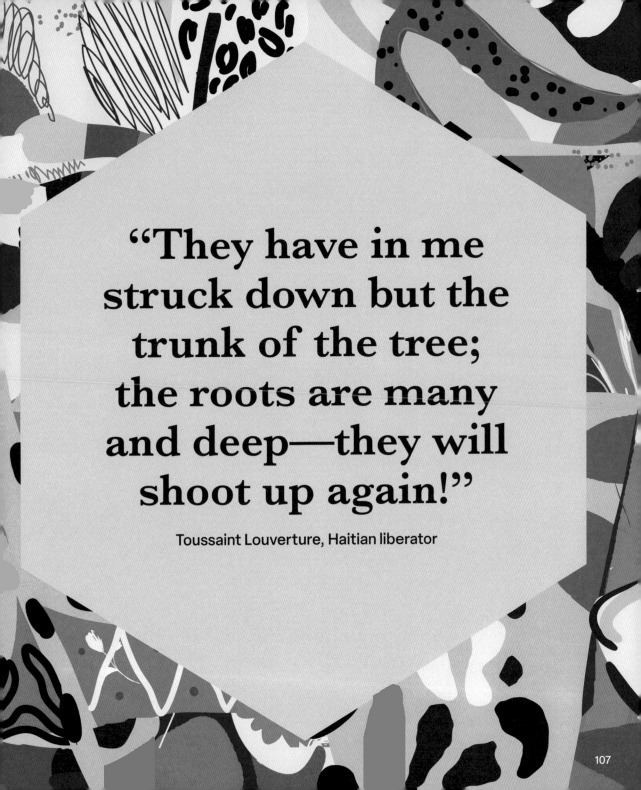

"They have in me struck down but the trunk of the tree; the roots are many and deep—they will shoot up again!"

Toussaint Louverture, Haitian liberator

Betty Shabazz (1934–1997) was an educator, orator, civil rights activist, and wife of Black nationalist and Pan Africanist leader Malcolm X. After the assassination of her husband in 1965, Shabazz struggled as a single mother. She went on to earn a PhD in education administration and defend the legacy of her husband, in effect creating her own legacy of struggle. She continued to contribute to Black movements and organizations and founded the Malcolm X Medical Scholarship Program as well as the Malcolm X Memorial Center. Shabazz is viewed as a dignitary among African American social movements and organizations. The Malcolm X and Dr. Betty Shabazz Memorial and Education Center (The Shabazz Center), in collaboration with Columbia University, was established in the Audubon Ballroom in New York in honor of the couple. The Shabazz Center is a cultural institution that cultivates racial and social justice movements.

"What should young people know about Malcolm? They should know about his internal strength and discipline and understand that a lot of people can climb the mountains, and deal with people on a very affluent level but don't understand what is happening in the valleys. And that if they are going to be future leaders that people are going to have to understand the diversity of people, ethnicity, political, religious."

Betty Shabazz, African American activist

Dudley Laws (1934–2011) was a prominent Jamaican Canadian social activist and human rights advocate in Toronto, Canada. He is best known for founding the Black Action Defence Committee (BADC) in 1988 and advocating for justice on behalf of Black Canadians facing discrimination within the legal system. Through his organizing initiatives, he mobilized hundreds of thousands of people to fight for social justice and civil rights. His legacy continues to be a source of inspiration for activists around the world, who strive to ensure that all people have access to justice and dignity. He passed away in 2011, but his memory lives on through those he inspired.

"The worst thing to do in life is to live in fear. I have no fear at all. If one becomes afraid, you can't do your work. You'll be looking over your shoulders and be afraid to say what you want to say."

Dudley Laws, Jamaican Canadian activist

Charlotte Maxeke (1871–1939) was a pioneering South African activist, educator, and clergywoman. She was an early leader in the struggle against racial segregation in South Africa, becoming the first Black South African woman to earn a university degree. A renowned orator and advocate for women's rights, Maxeke founded the Bantu Women's League and was a prominent figure in South African politics throughout her lifetime. The Charlotte Maxeke Johannesburg Academic Hospital was renamed in her honor. Maxeke's pioneering work and tireless activism provided an invaluable basis for the civil rights of all South Africans, something she had dedicated her life to achieving.

"This work is not ourselves. Kill that spirit of 'self' and do not live above your people. If you can rise, bring some with you. Circulate your work and distribute as much information as possible, because this is not your Council, but the Council of African women from here to Egypt. Do away with fearful jealousy, kill that spirit and love one another as brothers and sisters. Stand by your motto: Do unto others as ye would that they should unto you."

Charlotte Maxeke, South African educator, known as the Mother of Black Freedom

James Weldon Johnson (1871–1938) was an African American author, civil rights activist, educator, lawyer, and diplomat. He is best known for writing the lyrics to the popular song "Lift Every Voice and Sing," which has become known as the Black national anthem. Johnson wrote many other notable works of poetry, fiction, and nonfiction during his lifetime. He also served as a leader of the NAACP and other progressive organizations striving to advance civil rights for African Americans in the early twentieth century. Johnson was an important figure in the Harlem Renaissance, advocating for literature and art that celebrated African American culture and history. His legacy continues to inspire generations of activists fighting for social justice today.

"Lift every voice and sing,

Till earth and heaven ring,

Ring with the harmonies of Liberty;

Let our rejoicing rise

High as the list'ning skies,

Let it resound loud as the rolling sea.

Sing a song full of the faith that the dark past has taught us,

Sing a song full of the hope that the present has brought us;

Facing the rising sun of our new day begun,

Let us march on till victory is won."

James Weldon Johnson, African American writer and civil rights leader

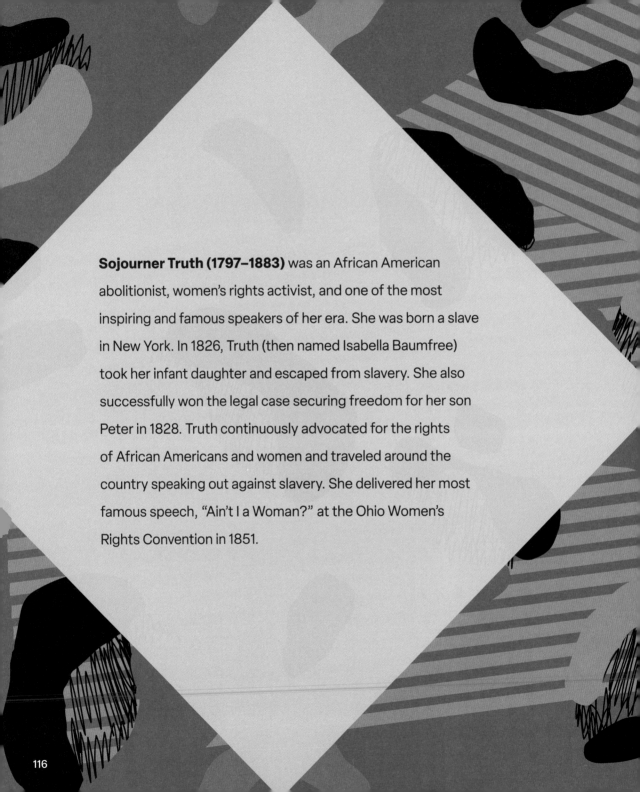

Sojourner Truth (1797–1883) was an African American abolitionist, women's rights activist, and one of the most inspiring and famous speakers of her era. She was born a slave in New York. In 1826, Truth (then named Isabella Baumfree) took her infant daughter and escaped from slavery. She also successfully won the legal case securing freedom for her son Peter in 1828. Truth continuously advocated for the rights of African Americans and women and traveled around the country speaking out against slavery. She delivered her most famous speech, "Ain't I a Woman?" at the Ohio Women's Rights Convention in 1851.

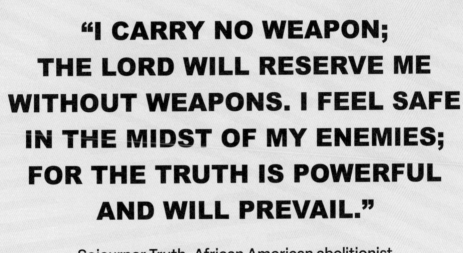

"I CARRY NO WEAPON;
THE LORD WILL RESERVE ME
WITHOUT WEAPONS. I FEEL SAFE
IN THE MIDST OF MY ENEMIES;
FOR THE TRUTH IS POWERFUL
AND WILL PREVAIL."

Sojourner Truth, African American abolitionist
and women's rights advocate

FREEDOM AND LIBERATION

The battle for freedom and liberation has been ongoing for people of the Pan African world, especially within the last four hundred years. Freedom is what we have always wanted. This includes in particular the freedom to live our lives in peace and raise our families without the harms of an unjust world. Over the last few centuries, Black people endured the transatlantic slave trade, also known as the Maafa. Consequently, centuries of enslavement have been countered with centuries of fighting for freedom, human rights, and self-preservation. We also endured colonization and are still grappling with its effects. During colonialism, the African continent was carved into territories under the rule of various European nations. African kingdoms and communities were subjected to violence, displacement, and loss of sovereignty. Still, colonization was met with fierce resistance. Africans and African descendants throughout the Pan African world organized and supported each other's efforts for freedom, eventually leading to the independence of African nations in the 1960s.

Freedom is more than a physical state; it is also a spiritual and mental state. It includes the freedom to love whom we want to love, pray how we want to pray, and express ourselves in any way that we desire. Our struggle for freedom and liberation has been a struggle to reassert our humanity in its totality, along with our right to survive and thrive.

The next sequence includes quotes that highlight our continued thirst for freedom and the ingenuity used to uplift our communities and bring us closer to a liberated future.

artist | Affen Segun, *Say It Out Loud IIII*

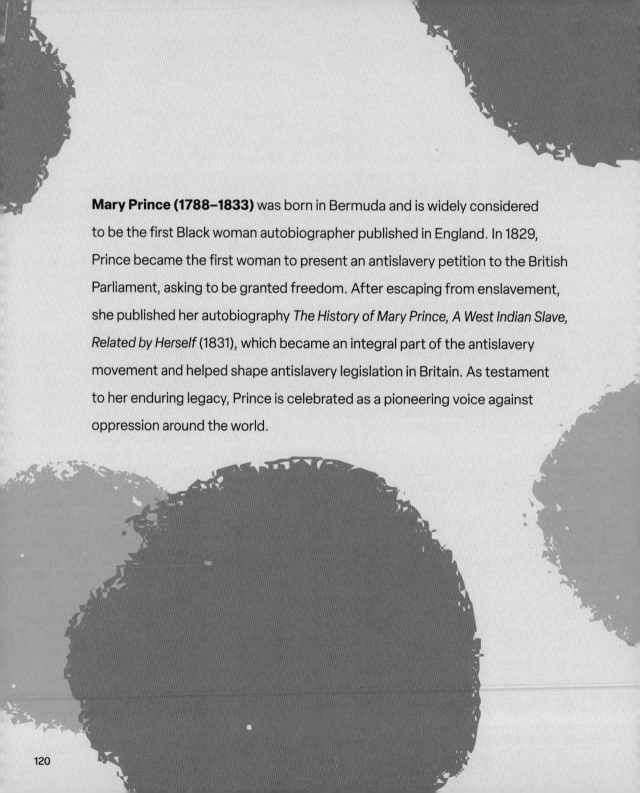

Mary Prince (1788–1833) was born in Bermuda and is widely considered to be the first Black woman autobiographer published in England. In 1829, Prince became the first woman to present an antislavery petition to the British Parliament, asking to be granted freedom. After escaping from enslavement, she published her autobiography *The History of Mary Prince, A West Indian Slave, Related by Herself* (1831), which became an integral part of the antislavery movement and helped shape antislavery legislation in Britain. As testament to her enduring legacy, Prince is celebrated as a pioneering voice against oppression around the world.

"All slaves want to be free—to be free is very sweet . . . I have been a slave myself—I know what slaves feel—I can tell by myself what other slaves feel, and by what they have told me. The man that says slaves be quite happy in slavery—that they don't want to be free—that man is either ignorant or a lying person. I never heard a slave say so. I never heard a Buckra man say so, till I heard tell of it in England. Such people ought to be ashamed of themselves."

Mary Prince, Black British author

Solomon Kalushi Mahlangu (1956–1979) was a South African anti-apartheid freedom fighter. He joined the African National Congress's military unit, uMkhonto weSizwe, in 1976 and became one of its most exemplary members. For his resistance to apartheid and activism, he was arrested and sentenced to death by the apartheid government in 1977, despite being only twenty-two years old. His execution caused a nationwide outcry and rallies were organized in response. This launched him into the collective national memory as an emblem of anti-apartheid protest and resistance. He has since been honored through numerous memorials and biographies, and the Solomon Mahlangu Freedom Square was named in his honor in Pretoria, South Africa. He is remembered today as a martyr for freedom and justice.

"My blood will nourish the tree that will bear the fruits of freedom. Tell my people that I love them. They must continue the fight."

Solomon Kalushi Mahlangu, South African freedom fighter and anti-apartheid activist

Claudia Jones (1915–1964) was a Trinidadian-born journalist, activist, and communist. She had an important influence on the United States civil rights movement, due to her work supporting the Black working class. In 1948, Jones was sentenced to prison for her involvement with the Communist Party USA. Deported from the United States in 1955, Jones became a major leader in the United Kingdom's early postwar civil rights movement and founded Britain's first major Black newspaper, *The West Indian Gazette.* Through her activism and writing, she advocated for the rights of the African diaspora and was a powerful advocate of socialist feminism. In 2008, Jones was featured on official United Kingdom postage stamps. She is celebrated every year as a cofounder of the Notting Hill Carnival, which commemorates Caribbean culture, music, and history. Her legacy continues through the Claudia Jones Organisation, which "supports African Caribbean women and families in Hackney and surrounding boroughs in London."

"A people's art is the genesis of their freedom."

Claudia Jones, Trinidadian American and Black British political activist

Fannie Lou Hamer (1917–1977) was an African American civil rights leader and voting rights activist. Born into poverty in rural Mississippi, she worked as a sharecropper and later as a civil rights organizer with the Student Nonviolent Coordinating Committee (SNCC). She cofounded the Mississippi Freedom Democratic Party and famously challenged the all-white Mississippi Democratic Party delegation at the Democratic National Convention. Hamer was an outspoken advocate for voting rights and other social justice issues, and her words became a rallying cry of the civil rights movement. Her activism earned her national recognition. She continued to fight for civil rights until her death in 1977. Her life and work remain an inspiration to millions today.

"Sometimes it seem like to tell the truth today is to run the risk of being killed. But if I fall while I'm in Kentucky, I'll fall five feet four inches forward in the fight for freedom. I'm not backing off."

Fannie Lou Hamer, African American activist

Samuel Sharpe (1801–1832) was an influential enslaved Jamaican activist and religious leader. He is best known for his role in sparking the 1831 Christmas Rebellion, a major uprising that helped lead to the end of slavery in Jamaica. Born into slavery in Montego Bay, Jamaica, Sharpe was raised in a Baptist household and was highly religious (serving as a deacon). Beginning in 1825, Sharpe organized meetings among enslaved Africans on plantations to discuss issues surrounding their treatment by their masters. After years of peaceful protests, Sharpe decided to lead a strike in December of 1831. The strike was known as the Christmas Rebellion or Baptist War, and it quickly spread throughout Jamaica, eventually leading to the British Parliament enacting legislation that would abolish slavery in Jamaica on August 1, 1834. Though Samuel Sharpe was hanged in 1832 for his participation in the rebellion, he was officially named a national hero of Jamaica in 1975.

"I would rather die upon yonder gallows than live in slavery."

Samuel Sharpe, Jamaican liberator and national hero

Ayọ Tometi (b. 1984) is a Nigerian American civil rights activist and former executive director of the Black Alliance for Just Immigration (BAJI). Born in Arizona to Nigerian immigrant parents, she grew up with a passion for social justice and education. She has dedicated her life to advocating for human rights, racial justice, and immigrants' rights. She organized against Arizona's SB 1070 anti-immigration law (2010). She is also a founding member of Black Lives Matter, an international movement focused on combating systemic racism and police brutality. Tometi has won numerous awards for her work, including being named one of *Time* magazine's 100 Most Influential People in 2020.

"We can't stop until we all get free. And we know that we can't get free until Black lives matter. And I know that we were all created to be alive in this time period for this specific work, no matter where we are, no matter your location. You have a set of experiences and gifts that we all need in order for us to get free."

Ayọ Tometi, Nigerian American activist and cofounder of Black Lives Matter

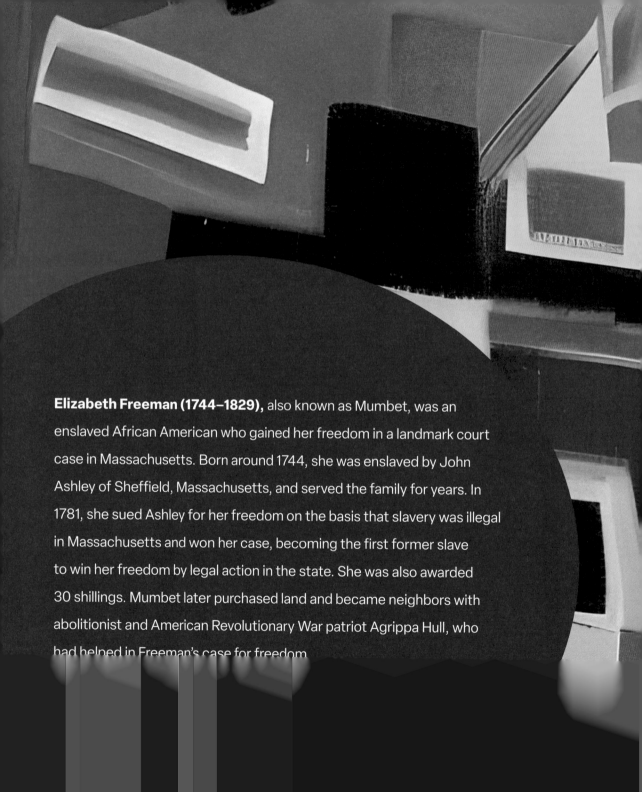

Elizabeth Freeman (1744–1829), also known as Mumbet, was an enslaved African American who gained her freedom in a landmark court case in Massachusetts. Born around 1744, she was enslaved by John Ashley of Sheffield, Massachusetts, and served the family for years. In 1781, she sued Ashley for her freedom on the basis that slavery was illegal in Massachusetts and won her case, becoming the first former slave to win her freedom by legal action in the state. She was also awarded 30 shillings. Mumbet later purchased land and became neighbors with abolitionist and American Revolutionary War patriot Agrippa Hull, who had helped in Freeman's case for freedom.

"Any time while I was a slave, if one minute's freedom had been offered to me, and I had been told I must die at the end of that minute, I would have taken it— just to stand one minute on God's earth a free woman—I would."

Elizabeth Freeman (Mumbet), African American activist

POLITICS

Politics have a major influence over our current realities and our prospects for the future. For people of the Pan African world, politics can make the difference between a thriving community and a community in turmoil. However, political parties, influence, and activism are delicate dances that are often frustrating and filled with disappointment. Yet tackling the political sphere is a necessary battle. Black communities need and deserve a voice in the policies that affect our lives. We need and deserve people-appointed representation that understands our concerns but also implements policies that radically change our lives for the better.

Dr. Martin Luther King Jr. advocated for civil and labor rights. This was activism but also a political push for positive change. Nelson Mandela fought against apartheid and endured unjust imprisonment, then went on to become the first Black president of South Africa—enacting policies to lead South Africa out of a period of mass subjugation to a period of freedom and people-led power. People of the Pan African world have often used political strategy to transform lives, communities, and nations. Through politics, we have the opportunity to structure societies that benefit the whole instead of an elite few.

The next sequence shares quotes from the African continent and the diaspora, showcasing the need for politics as a tool for changemaking, inclusion, and mobilization.

artist | Uzo Njoku, *My Black Perspective*

Jesse Jackson (b. 1941) is an African American civil rights activist, politician, and minister. He is known for his work to end segregation and advance social justice through nonviolent means. He founded the Rainbow/PUSH Coalition in 1971, which works on issues of health care, education, economic development, and other causes affecting African Americans and underrepresented groups. Throughout his career, he has advocated for equal rights, voting rights, and access to public services. He is a powerful voice advocating for greater economic and educational opportunities for those who have been historically marginalized in communities across the United States. Jackson ran for president of the United States in 1984 and 1988. In the 2000s, he continued his activism by focusing on global issues such as poverty, AIDS, human rights, and racism. His career spans five decades of political involvement and continues to this day.

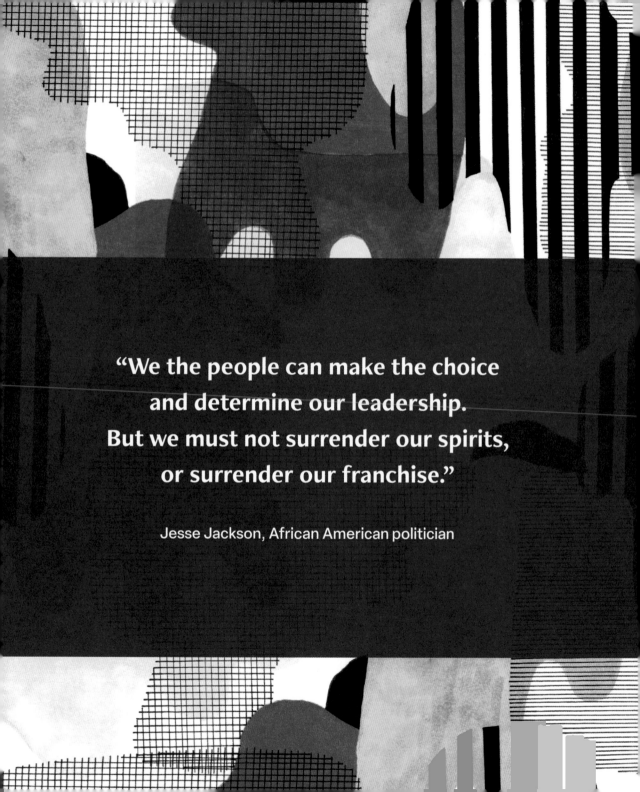

"We the people can make the choice
and determine our leadership.
But we must not surrender our spirits,
or surrender our franchise."

Jesse Jackson, African American politician

Frederick Douglass (1818–1895) was an African American abolitionist, orator, writer, and statesman. Born into slavery in Maryland, he became a self-emancipated slave as a young man and threw himself wholeheartedly into the struggle for civil rights for African Americans. He was a powerful voice in the abolitionist movement and spoke out widely against the evils of slavery, both in the United States and around the world. After his escape from bondage, he became an influential leader in the antislavery movement, speaking to large crowds across America and Great Britain. During his life, Douglass wrote three autobiographies that were essential to the fight for social justice. He also founded *The North Star*, the first antislavery newspaper, in 1847. He was a tireless advocate for the rights of African Americans, and he is remembered today as one of the most influential figures in American history.

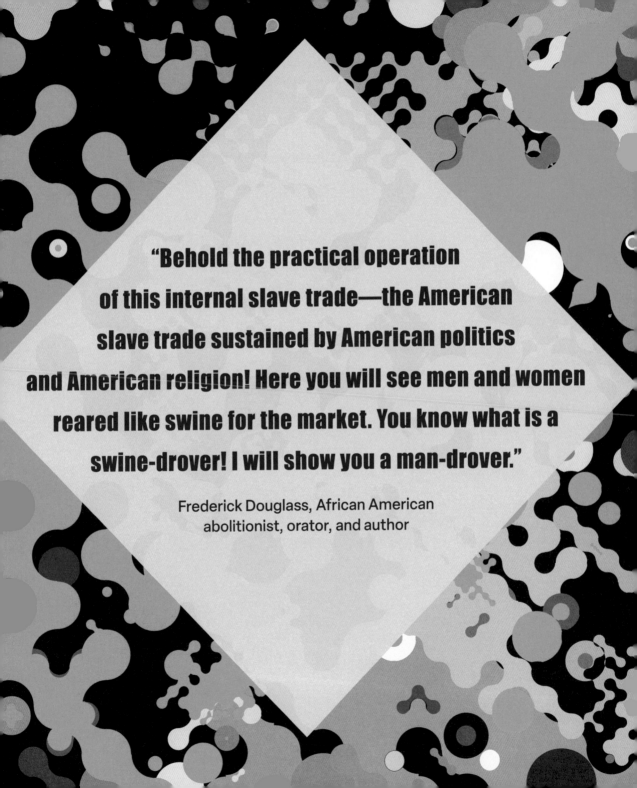

"Behold the practical operation of this internal slave trade—the American slave trade sustained by American politics and American religion! Here you will see men and women reared like swine for the market. You know what is a swine-drover! I will show you a man-drover."

Frederick Douglass, African American abolitionist, orator, and author

Francia Márquez (b. 1981) is a Colombian human rights activist who works to protect the environment and Indigenous peoples in her home country. She received the Goldman Environmental Prize in 2018 for her fight against large-scale, open-pit gold-mining operations that have caused extensive water and air pollution in the areas where she lives and works. Márquez has become an internationally recognized leader advocating for new laws and policies that protect Indigenous rights as well as providing legal assistance to those who have been harmed by mining operations. She continues to be a strong voice in both Colombia and around the world, fighting for justice and sustainability. In 2022, Márquez became the vice president of Colombia.

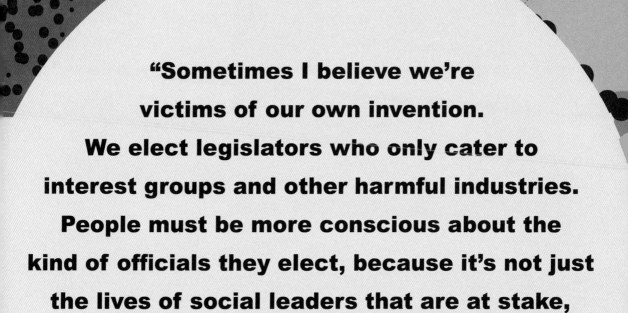

"Sometimes I believe we're victims of our own invention. We elect legislators who only cater to interest groups and other harmful industries. People must be more conscious about the kind of officials they elect, because it's not just the lives of social leaders that are at stake, but the very existence of humanity today."

Francia Márquez, Afro-Colombian politician and 13th vice president of Colombia

Barack Hussein Obama II (b. 1961) served as the 44th president of the United States from 2009 to 2017. He was the first African American to hold the office, previously serving as a United States senator representing Illinois and before that as a member of the Illinois State Senate. Obama is known for signing comprehensive health care reform legislation, negotiating international agreements such as the Paris Agreement, strengthening relationships with Cuba, and establishing the Deferred Action for Childhood Arrivals (DACA) program. Additionally, Obama's presidency was marked by initiatives such as the expansion of LGBTQ+ rights, an increase in government transparency, and the implementation of new environmental regulations.

"Our youth, our drive, our diversity and openness, our boundless capacity for risk and reinvention means that the future should be ours. But that potential will only be realized if our democracy works. Only if our politics better reflects the decency of our people."

Barack Obama, 44th president of the United States and the first Black American president

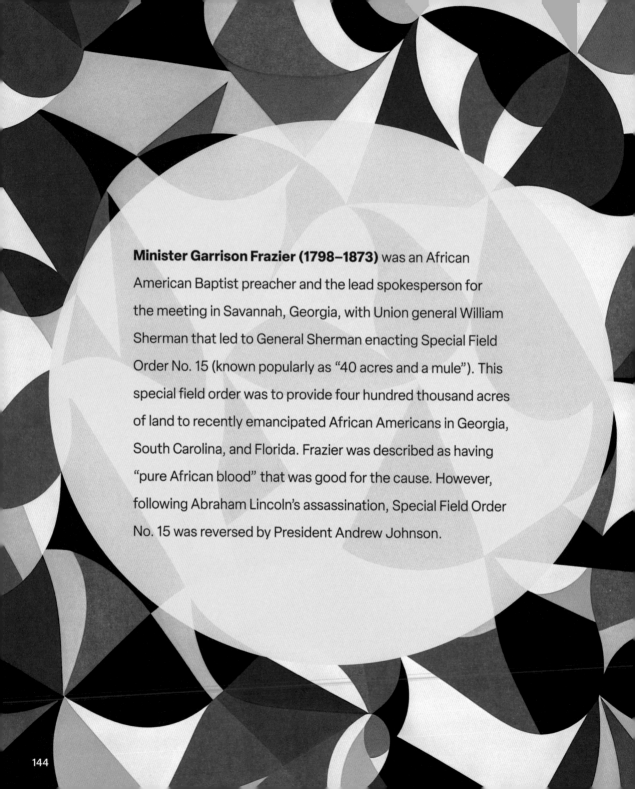

Minister Garrison Frazier (1798–1873) was an African American Baptist preacher and the lead spokesperson for the meeting in Savannah, Georgia, with Union general William Sherman that led to General Sherman enacting Special Field Order No. 15 (known popularly as "40 acres and a mule"). This special field order was to provide four hundred thousand acres of land to recently emancipated African Americans in Georgia, South Carolina, and Florida. Frazier was described as having "pure African blood" that was good for the cause. However, following Abraham Lincoln's assassination, Special Field Order No. 15 was reversed by President Andrew Johnson.

"THE WAY WE CAN BEST TAKE CARE OF OURSELVES IS TO HAVE LAND, AND TURN IT AND TILL IT BY OUR OWN LABOR—THAT IS, BY THE LABOR OF THE WOMEN AND CHILDREN AND OLD MEN; AND WE CAN SOON MAINTAIN OURSELVES AND HAVE SOMETHING TO SPARE. AND TO ASSIST THE GOVERNMENT, THE YOUNG MEN SHOULD ENLIST IN THE SERVICE OF THE GOVERNMENT, AND SERVE IN SUCH MANNER AS THEY MAY BE WANTED."

Garrison Frazier, African American Baptist minister

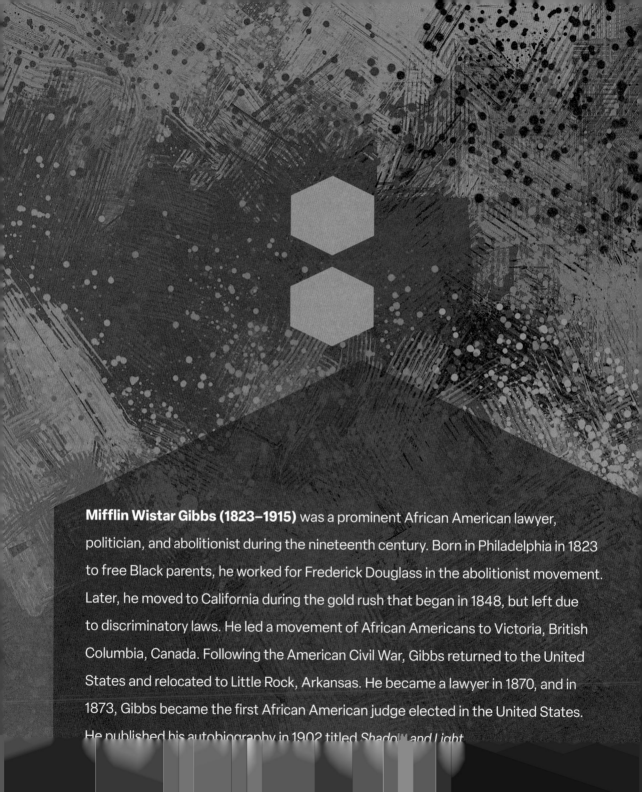

Mifflin Wistar Gibbs (1823–1915) was a prominent African American lawyer, politician, and abolitionist during the nineteenth century. Born in Philadelphia in 1823 to free Black parents, he worked for Frederick Douglass in the abolitionist movement. Later, he moved to California during the gold rush that began in 1848, but left due to discriminatory laws. He led a movement of African Americans to Victoria, British Columbia, Canada. Following the American Civil War, Gibbs returned to the United States and relocated to Little Rock, Arkansas. He became a lawyer in 1870, and in 1873, Gibbs became the first African American judge elected in the United States. He published his autobiography in 1902 titled *Shadow and Light*.

"We have a deal of 'gush' about recognition. A demand for recognition presupposes a rightful claim based upon an inherent interest—deportment, special fitness, or legal right. In politics we rightfully claim recognition in the ratio of our numerical contribution to the body politic, and from public carriers, for the reason of performance of our part of the contract."

Mifflin Wistar Gibbs, African American lawyer and judge

BLACKNESS

There was a time when "Black" or "Blackness" was depicted as negative and something to shy away from. Blackness was something that we were meant to be ashamed of, according to the Western world. However, during the 1960s and 1970s, many people of the Pan African world began to embrace Blackness as a source of pride. For them, Blackness became a signal of perseverance in the face of struggle. What was once meant to subjugate us, through the weaponization of race, became a tool for Pan African organizing. Blackness and Black identity became more than a racial descriptor. It became a political perspective. Activists like Kwame Ture (Stokely Carmichael) and Steve Biko highlighted the political aspects of Blackness and utilized it to critique and overcome unjust systems. Blackness became a rallying cry for people of African descent. It became a focal point for organizing and unification.

Even Dr. Martin Luther King Jr. highlighted the negative ways in which Blackness was framed in mainstream society and encouraged his listeners to realize that these negative perceptions were built on lies. Musical artists like Nina Simone, Miriam Makeba, Celia Cruz, and James Brown used their celebrity and musical talents to promote the joys and pride of Blackness culturally. Publications like *Jet* magazine began to publish Beauty of the Week. Blackness became beautiful, and this beauty is connected to our histories, cultures, and African ancestry.

People of African descent of various skin tones continue to face colorism, racism, and prejudice. However, after centuries of negative depictions and discrimination, current generations are now able to look at the works of past political and cultural activists, who taught us to embrace being ourselves and dare to love ourselves as Black people.

artist | Rendani Nemakhavhani, *A WL Girlie*

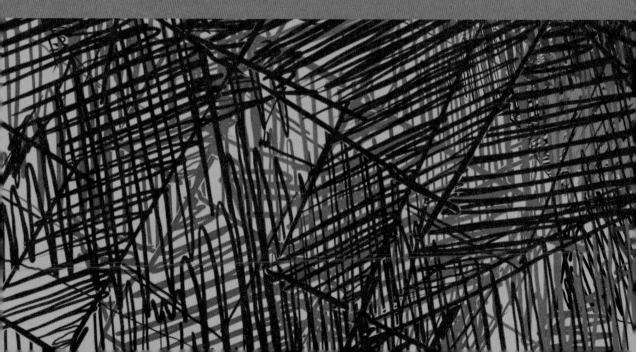

Agrippa Hull (1759–1848) was a Revolutionary War veteran and the most highly decorated African American soldier of his time. Hull was born free in Massachusetts. His father was said to be an African prince. He served in the Continental Army, joining shortly after his eighteenth birthday, as an orderly to General John Paterson and aide to Tadeusz Kościuszko during and following the American Revolutionary War. He was an abolitionist who advocated for the freedom of African Americans. He also helped the legal case of Elizabeth Freeman (Mumbet), who successfully sued her "master" and gained freedom. They later became neighbors. Hull used his earnings to purchase various plots of land, eventually becoming the largest landowner of African descent in Stockbridge, Massachusetts.

"It is not the cover of the book, but what the book contains is the question. Many a good book has dark covers. Which is the worst, the white Black man or the Black white man? To be Black outside, or to be Black inside?"

Agrippa Hull, African American Revolutionary War hero

Rosa Clemente (b. 1972) is an Afro–Puerto Rican activist, public speaker, and political organizer. She is a longtime community advocate and serves as the founder of PR (Puerto Rico) on the Map, a grassroots organization that promotes the political empowerment of Puerto Ricans both on the island and in the diaspora. She is a graduate of the University of Albany and obtained her master's from Cornell University in Africana studies. She was a pivotal organizer of the National Hip Hop Political Convention, among other organizations. In 2008, she was chosen by the Green Party to be their vice-presidential running mate alongside Cynthia McKinney. Clemente continues to be an inspirational advocate for social and racial justice.

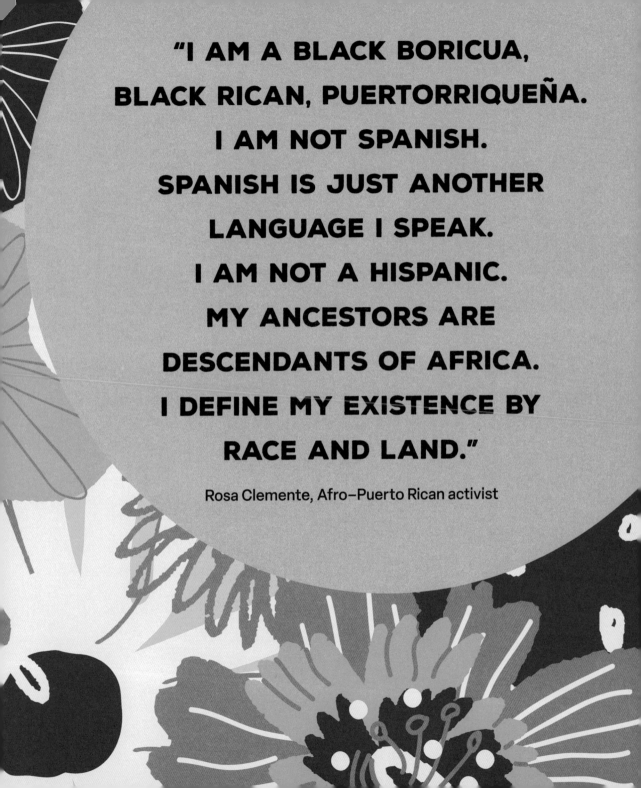

"I AM A BLACK BORICUA, BLACK RICAN, PUERTORRIQUEÑA. I AM NOT SPANISH. SPANISH IS JUST ANOTHER LANGUAGE I SPEAK. I AM NOT A HISPANIC. MY ANCESTORS ARE DESCENDANTS OF AFRICA. I DEFINE MY EXISTENCE BY RACE AND LAND."

Rosa Clemente, Afro–Puerto Rican activist

Walter Rodney (1942–1980) was a prominent Guyanese Pan Africanist scholar, historian, and political activist. He was widely known for his influential writings on African history and the development of postcolonial Caribbean nations. His book, *How Europe Underdeveloped Africa* (1972), is considered an Africana and Pan Africanist studies classic. It critically examines the economic exploitation of Africa by European powers. Rodney was a vocal champion of Pan Africanism and dedicated his life to liberating African people from the oppressive systems of colonialism and imperialism. He was tragically assassinated in 1980 at the age of thirty-eight, but his writings remain an important source of inspiration for many activists around the world.

"The Black intellectual, the Black academic, must attach himself to the activity of the Black masses."

Walter Rodney, Guyanese Pan African scholar and activist

Katharina Oguntoye (b. 1959) is an Afro-German feminist, political activist, and professor of Nigerian heritage. She is founder of the Joliba Interkulturelles Netzwerk (JOLIBA, Intercultural Network in Berlin), which fosters cross-cultural affairs and advocates for Afro-German families. Her activism focuses on the liberation and rights of Afro-descended families and women in Germany and beyond. Her seminal works on the lives of Afro-Germans include *Stellt euch einander und der Welt vor* (*Introduce Yourself to Each Other and the World*, c. 1984) and *Farbe bekennen* (*Showing Our Colors: Afro-German Women Speak Out*, 1986). She also cofounded the Initiative Schwarze Menschen in Deutschland (Initiative of Black People in Germany). Her work has been used as an example for Afro-German families overcoming oppression and marginalization in German society.

"When we met with about
30 people in the 'Black Germans'
initiative, we mainly discussed
topics such as what does
it actually mean to be
Afro-German in our lives?
First, we agreed on this term,
but then we also discussed
in the group why some
people prefer to say Black
Germans because they don't
want to refer to their African
background but to their
American background.
We then said that both are
possible, but that none of us
will accept the 'N-word.' "

Katharina Oguntoye, Afro-German writer,
historian, activist, and poet

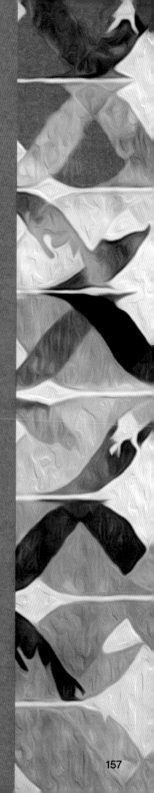

Joseph Seamon Cotter Jr. (1895–1919) was an African American playwright, poet, and writer from Louisville, Kentucky. He was the son of the prominent African American playwright Joseph Seamon Cotter Sr. He attended Fisk University but was unable to complete his studies due to illness. He wrote poetry and plays, including *On the Fields of France* (published posthumously in 1920). He died of tuberculosis at the young age of twenty-four. His poetry was featured in James Weldon Johnson's *The Book of American Negro Poetry* (1922). Following his death, his father continued to promote and publish his work.

"Is It Because I Am Black?
Why do men smile when I speak,
And call my speech
The whimperings of a babe
That cries but knows not
what it wants?
Is it because I am Black?

Why do men sneer when I arise
And stand in their councils,
And look them eye to eye,
And speak their tongue?
Is it because I am Black?"

Joseph Seamon Cotter Jr., African American playwright,
poet, and writer

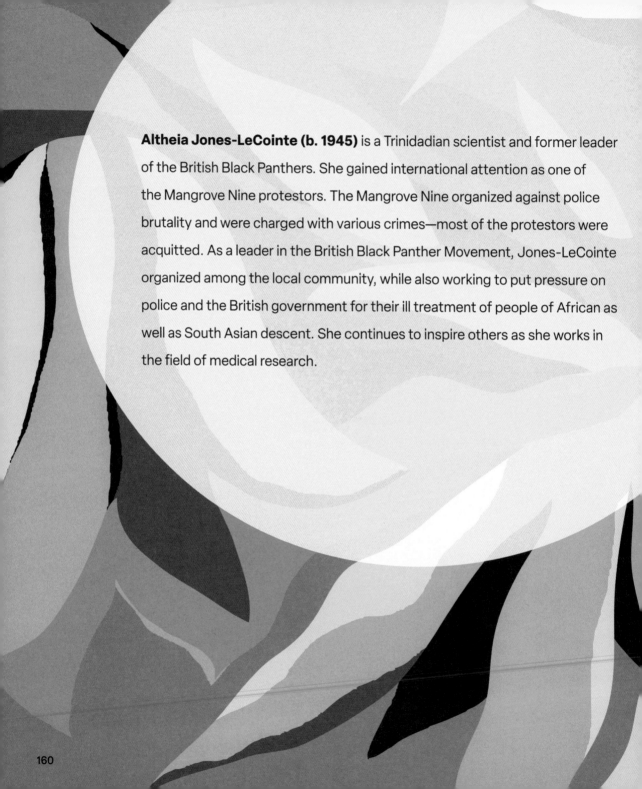

Altheia Jones-LeCointe (b. 1945) is a Trinidadian scientist and former leader of the British Black Panthers. She gained international attention as one of the Mangrove Nine protestors. The Mangrove Nine organized against police brutality and were charged with various crimes—most of the protestors were acquitted. As a leader in the British Black Panther Movement, Jones-LeCointe organized among the local community, while also working to put pressure on police and the British government for their ill treatment of people of African as well as South Asian descent. She continues to inspire others as she works in the field of medical research.

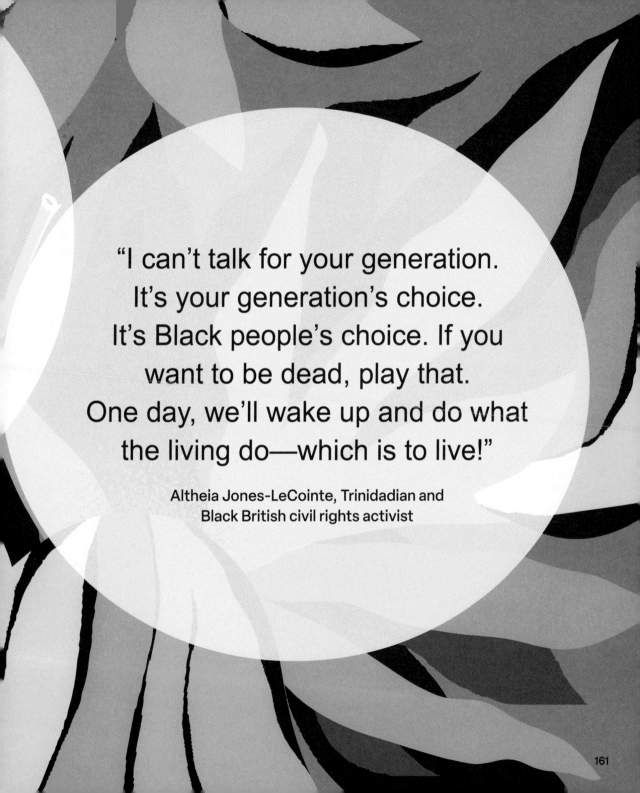

"I can't talk for your generation.
It's your generation's choice.
It's Black people's choice. If you
want to be dead, play that.
One day, we'll wake up and do what
the living do—which is to live!"

Altheia Jones-LeCointe, Trinidadian and
Black British civil rights activist

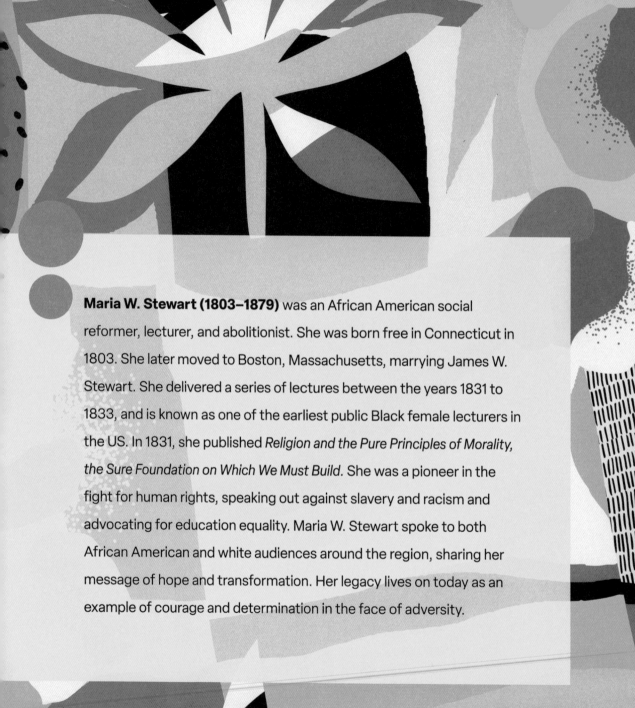

Maria W. Stewart (1803–1879) was an African American social reformer, lecturer, and abolitionist. She was born free in Connecticut in 1803. She later moved to Boston, Massachusetts, marrying James W. Stewart. She delivered a series of lectures between the years 1831 to 1833, and is known as one of the earliest public Black female lecturers in the US. In 1831, she published *Religion and the Pure Principles of Morality, the Sure Foundation on Which We Must Build.* She was a pioneer in the fight for human rights, speaking out against slavery and racism and advocating for education equality. Maria W. Stewart spoke to both African American and white audiences around the region, sharing her message of hope and transformation. Her legacy lives on today as an example of courage and determination in the face of adversity.

"It is not the color of the skin that makes the man or the woman, but the principle formed in the soul. Brilliant wit will shine, come from whence it will; and genius and talent will not hide the brightness of its lustre."

Maria W. Stewart, African American lecturer and abolitionist

Anita Scott Coleman (1890–1960)
was an African American and Afro-Mexican poet and writer during the Harlem Renaissance. She was born in Guaymas, Sonora, in Mexico, to Buffalo Soldier William Henry Scott and his formerly enslaved wife, Mary Ann. (Buffalo Soldiers were African American soldiers who served in Western states on the American frontier during the nineteenth century.) Coleman was raised in New Mexico. In 1909, she graduated from New Mexico State Teachers College (now known as Western New Mexico University). In 1916, she married printer James Harold Coleman. They went on to have five children. Her poetry was featured in James Weldon Johnson's *The Book of American Negro Poetry* (1922). Coleman's short stories were later collected and published posthumously under the title *Unfinished Masterpiece: The Harlem Renaissance Fiction of Anita Scott Coleman* (2008).

"God is African—for night is robed in black. The twinkling stars are Black men's eyes. The black clouds, tempests tell. While little seeds of flowers birthed are Tans and brown and black."

Anita Scott Coleman, African American and Afro-Mexican poet and writer

PAN AFRICANISM

Pan Africanism embraces the interconnectedness of the Pan African world, focusing on Africans and people of African descent throughout the diaspora. Though many of us have been displaced and relocated through the perils of the transatlantic slave trade and colonialism, many of our ancestors and elders held on to the belief and idea that people of the Pan African world should reunify and build connections internationally. Historically, Pan Africanists have challenged oppressive systems, advocated for civil rights, and led independence movements. Many of the leading Black historical figures of Black liberation movements maintained a Pan Africanist ideology, understanding that what affects the lives of African people in one place affects us all, regardless of where we are located. Pan Africanist ideologies permeated the works of W. E. B. Du Bois, Anna Julia Cooper, Martin R. Delany, Marcus Garvey, Amy Jacques Garvey, Amy Ashwood Garvey, Walter Rodney, Kwame Nkrumah, Malcolm X, and many others.

Many African descendants within the diaspora recognized the need for Pan African collaboration after spending centuries dealing with racism and prejudice in the Americas. Similarly, African leaders on the continent promoted Pan Africanism after dealing with decades of European colonialism and centuries of political disruption. In 1900, descendants from the Pan African world came together for the first Pan African Conference held in London. It was organized by Trinidadian lawyer Henry Sylvester Williams. Over the last century, the tradition has continued, with a total of eight Pan African Congresses held so far.

The next sequence includes quotes from Black historical figures, activists, and scholars that define Pan Africanism and uplift the necessity of Pan Africanism for our collective survival.

artist | Gilles Mayk Navangi, *Elleux*

Robert Sobukwe (1924–1978) was a South African political activist and president of the Pan Africanist Congress (PAC). He is remembered for his leadership during the anti-apartheid movement, particularly anti-pass protests. These protests opposed the way Black South Africans were subject to passes they were mandated to carry by law and which strictly limited their movement for the purposes of segregation and apartheid. Sobukwe was also an editor of *The Africanist*, a publication of the PAC that focused on liberation. Following anti-pass protests and the Sharpeville massacre, Sobukwe was arrested and imprisoned by South Africa's apartheid government, sentenced to an indefinite detention that included six years in Robben Island Prison. After prison, he was subject to a government ban and permanent house arrest. He died in 1978 at the age of fifty-nine.

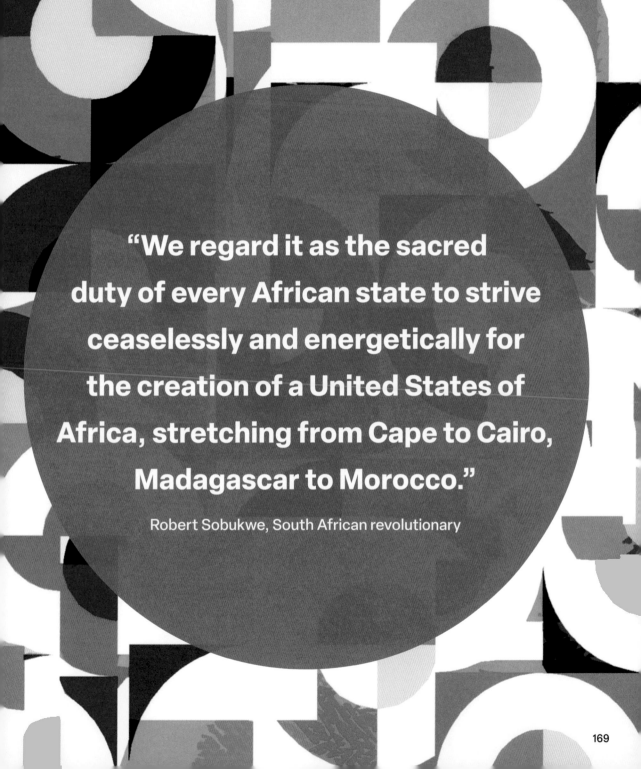

"We regard it as the sacred duty of every African state to strive ceaselessly and energetically for the creation of a United States of Africa, stretching from Cape to Cairo, Madagascar to Morocco."

Robert Sobukwe, South African revolutionary

Audley Moore (1898–1997) was a reparations activist and leader in the struggle to secure economic, political, and social justice for the Pan African world. Known as Queen Mother Moore, she advocated for reparations as a solution to the lasting legacy of enslavement and white supremacy. Moore played an instrumental role in the founding of a number of organizations dedicated to the fight for reparative justice, including the Republic of New Afrika and the National Coalition of Blacks for Reparations in America. She also founded the Universal Association of Ethiopian Women and the Committee for Reparations for Descendants of US Slaves. Her legacy will long be remembered as a powerful advocate for Pan African rights and reparations.

"I don't pay those borders no mind at all."

Audley "Queen Mother" Moore, mother of the modern-day reparations movement

Amy Euphemia Jacques Garvey (1895–1973) was a prominent Jamaican-born Pan Africanist, journalist, and civil rights activist in the early twentieth century. She was an advocate for women's rights and was one of the most active figures in the Universal Negro Improvement Association (UNIA) led by her husband, Marcus Garvey. Throughout her life she wrote extensively on Black liberation, Pan African freedom, and women's rights, editing and writing for *The Negro World* (the official newspaper of the UNIA). She was an inspiring leader who dedicated her life to the cause of self-determination for people of African descent worldwide. She continues to be a major influence for many today.

"Africa must be for Africans, and Negroes everywhere must be independent, God being our guide."

Amy Jacques Garvey, Jamaican Pan Africanist, UNIA leader, and editor of *The Negro World*

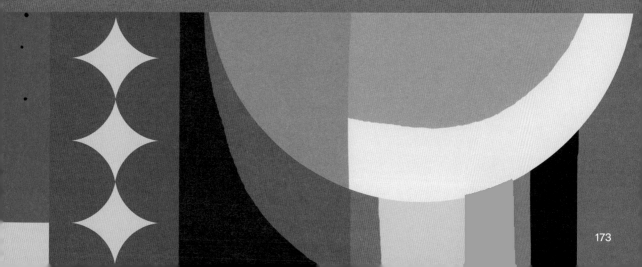

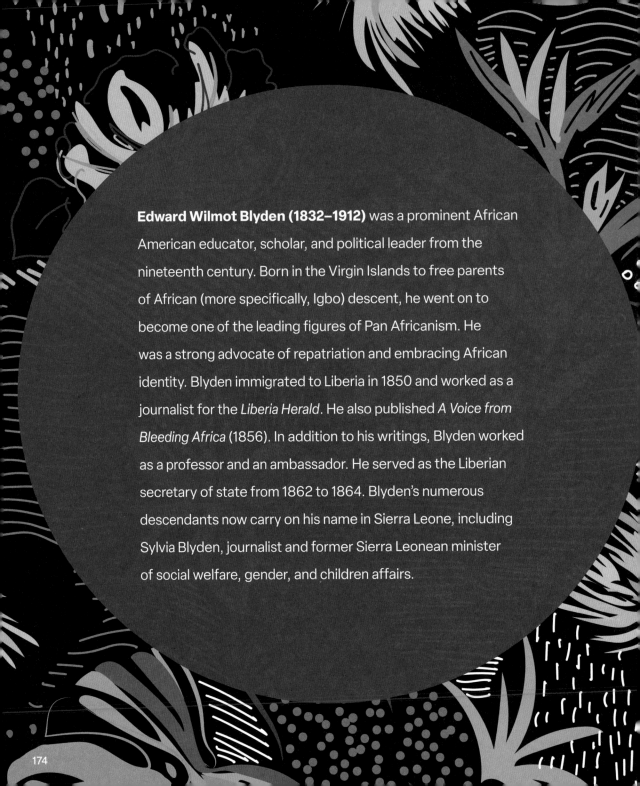

Edward Wilmot Blyden (1832–1912) was a prominent African American educator, scholar, and political leader from the nineteenth century. Born in the Virgin Islands to free parents of African (more specifically, Igbo) descent, he went on to become one of the leading figures of Pan Africanism. He was a strong advocate of repatriation and embracing African identity. Blyden immigrated to Liberia in 1850 and worked as a journalist for the *Liberia Herald*. He also published *A Voice from Bleeding Africa* (1856). In addition to his writings, Blyden worked as a professor and an ambassador. He served as the Liberian secretary of state from 1862 to 1864. Blyden's numerous descendants now carry on his name in Sierra Leone, including Sylvia Blyden, journalist and former Sierra Leonean minister of social welfare, gender, and children affairs.

"Africa may yet prove to be the spiritual conservatory of the world . . . When the civilized nations in consequence of their wonderful material development, shall have had their spiritual susceptibilities blunted through the agency of a captivating and absorbing materialism, it may be that they have to resort to Africa to recover some of the simple elements of faith."

Edward Wilmot Blyden, Liberian educator and the father of Pan Africanism

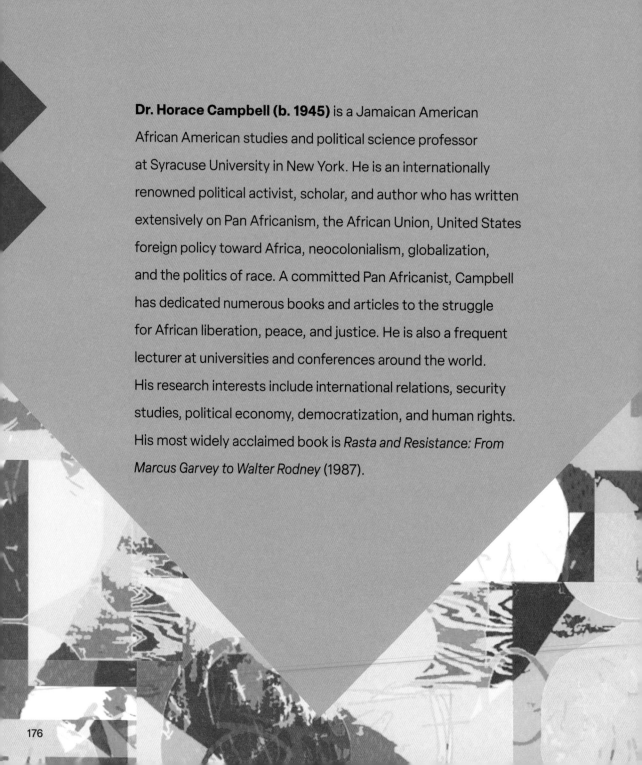

Dr. Horace Campbell (b. 1945) is a Jamaican American African American studies and political science professor at Syracuse University in New York. He is an internationally renowned political activist, scholar, and author who has written extensively on Pan Africanism, the African Union, United States foreign policy toward Africa, neocolonialism, globalization, and the politics of race. A committed Pan Africanist, Campbell has dedicated numerous books and articles to the struggle for African liberation, peace, and justice. He is also a frequent lecturer at universities and conferences around the world. His research interests include international relations, security studies, political economy, democratization, and human rights. His most widely acclaimed book is *Rasta and Resistance: From Marcus Garvey to Walter Rodney* (1987).

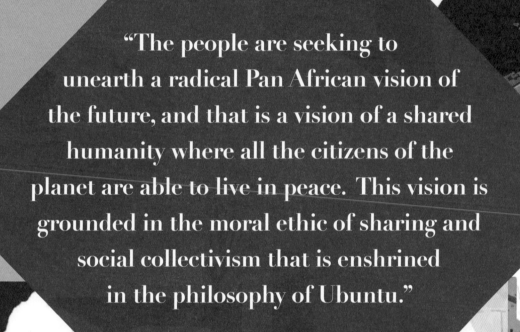

"The people are seeking to unearth a radical Pan African vision of the future, and that is a vision of a shared humanity where all the citizens of the planet are able to live in peace. This vision is grounded in the moral ethic of sharing and social collectivism that is enshrined in the philosophy of Ubuntu."

Horace Campbell, Jamaican American Pan Africanist and scholar

Martin R. Delany (1812–1885) was born free in Charles Town, a city in what is now West Virginia. After moving to Pittsburgh, Delany aided and treated African Americans during the cholera epidemic of the mid-1800s as a physician's assistant. In 1850, he was admitted to Harvard Medical School; however, he was denied an education there due to racial discrimination. Delany recruited for the United States Colored Troops during the American Civil War and became a field grade officer, the first African American to serve in this capacity in the United States Army. Delany was an advocate of African American emigration to Africa and wrote "Political Destiny of the Colored Race on the American Continent" in 1854, which advocated for emigration. The phrase "Africa for the Africans" is often attributed to him. This phrase was later popularized by Marcus Garvey and the United Negro Improvement Association (UNIA).

"From the earliest period of the history of nations, the African race had been known as an industrious people, cultivators of the soil. The grain fields of Ethiopia and Egypt were the themes of the poet, and their garners, the subject of the historian. Like the present America, all the world went to Africa, to get a supply of commodities. Their massive piles of masonry, their skilful architecture, their subterranean vaults, their deep and mysterious wells, their extensive artificial channels, their mighty sculptured solid rocks, and provinces of stone quarries; gave indisputable evidence, of the hardihood of that race of people."

Martin R. Delany, Pan African leader, Black nationalist, and abolitionist

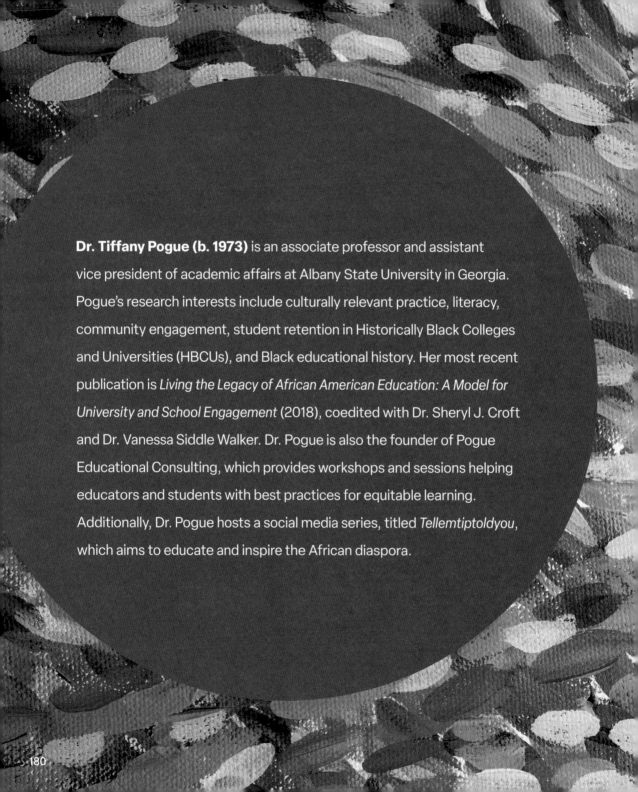

Dr. Tiffany Pogue (b. 1973) is an associate professor and assistant vice president of academic affairs at Albany State University in Georgia. Pogue's research interests include culturally relevant practice, literacy, community engagement, student retention in Historically Black Colleges and Universities (HBCUs), and Black educational history. Her most recent publication is *Living the Legacy of African American Education: A Model for University and School Engagement* (2018), coedited with Dr. Sheryl J. Croft and Dr. Vanessa Siddle Walker. Dr. Pogue is also the founder of Pogue Educational Consulting, which provides workshops and sessions helping educators and students with best practices for equitable learning. Additionally, Dr. Pogue hosts a social media series, titled *Tellemtiptoldyou*, which aims to educate and inspire the African diaspora.

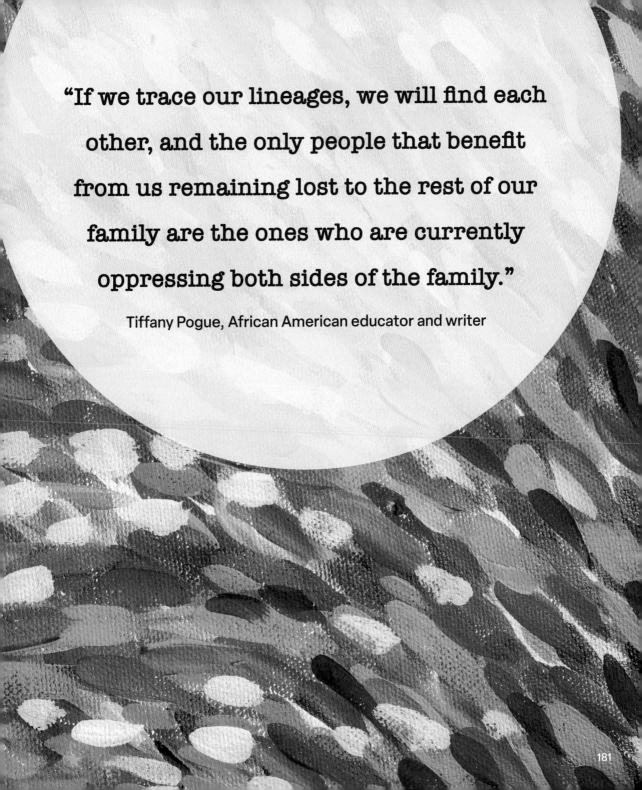

"If we trace our lineages, we will find each other, and the only people that benefit from us remaining lost to the rest of our family are the ones who are currently oppressing both sides of the family."

Tiffany Pogue, African American educator and writer

INDEX OF INDIVIDUALS

PERMISSIONS

CULTURE AND HISTORY

Hugh Masekela via *The Guardian*. "Hugh Masekela—What I'm thinking About . . . A Crisis for African Culture." March 12, 2013. Copyright Guardian News & Media Ltd 2023. https://www.theguardian.com/music/2013/mar/12/hugh-masekela-womadelaide-african-culture.

Werewere Liking via Michelle Mielly. "An Interview with Werewere Liking at the Ki-Yi Village, Abidjan, Côte d'Ivoire, 2 June 2002." *African Postcolonial Literature in the Postcolonial Web*. June 2, 2002. http://www.postcolonialweb.org/africa/cameroon/liking/2.html.

EDUCATION AND KNOWLEDGE

Mīcere Gīthae Mūgo via the Royal African Society. "Interview with Africa Writes Lifetime Achievement Award Winner Mīcere Gīthae Mūgo." *Royal African Society*. February 23, 2022. https://royalafricansociety.org/interview-with-africa-writes-lifetime-achievement-award-winner-micere-githae-mugo.

Na'im Akbar via Mind Productions and Associates. *Breaking the Chains of Psychological Slavery*. Tallahassee, FL: Mind Productions and Associates, 1996.

JUSTICE, CIVIL RIGHTS, AND HUMAN RIGHTS

Nigel Westmaas. "Hamilton College, the Question of 'Civility' and the Nation." *The Spectator*. September 19, 2019. https://spec.hamilton.edu/hamilton-college-the-question-of-civility-and-the-nation-140b540d4a5e.

RACE AND RACISM

Farai Chideya. *Don't Believe the Hype: Fighting Cultural Misinformation about African-Americans*. New York: Plume Books, 1995.

Kimani Nehusi. "Writing the History of Villages in Guyana and the Caribbean." *The History Gazette*, no. 71 (1994). https://www.yumpu.com/en/document/read/54469851/writing-the-history-of-villages-in-guyana-and-the-caribbean-by-kimani-nehusi.

Paul Stephenson via *The Guardian*. "Paul Stephenson: The Hero Who Refused to Leave a Pub—and Helped Desegregate Britain." October 1, 2020. Copyright Guardian News & Media Ltd, 2023. https://www.theguardian.com/society/2020/oct/01/paul-stephenson-the-hero-who-refused-to-leave-a-pub-and-helped-desegregate-britain.

GENDER, FEMINISM, AND WOMANISM

The Combahee River Collective via Zillah Eisenstein. *Capitalist Patriarchy and the Case for Socialist Feminism*. New York: Monthly Review Press, 1978.

Dwayne Wong (Omowale). "Women in Togo's Revolution and the Global African Revolution." *HuffPost* (Contributor Platform). November 20, 2017. https://www.huffpost.com/entry/women-in-togos-revolution-and-the-global-african-revolution_b_5a13756ae4b010527d677fc0.

PEACE AND LOVE

Basetsana Kumalo via Penguin Random House South Africa. *Bassie: My Journey of Hope*. Cape Town: Penguin Random House South Africa, 2019.

Harper Glenn via *Writer Unboxed*. "Interview with Harper Glenn." *Writer Unboxed*. October 4, 2022. https://writerunboxed.com/2022/10/04/interview-with-harper-glenn.

INSPIRATION, HOPE, AND PERSEVERANCE

Betty Shabazz via the Henry Hampton Collection, Washington University Libraries. *Eyes on the Prize II*. Boston: Blackside Inc., 1988.

Charlotte Mannya-Maxeke via the Charlotte Mannya-Maxeke Institute. Speech delivered at the National Council of African Women in 1938. The Charlotte Mannya-Maxeke Institute (CMMI) is a family initiative born out of the desire to preserve, promote, elevate and leverage the legacy left behind by Mme Charlotte. The CMMI was founded by three families related to this icon, namely the Maxekes, the Mannyas, and the Makhanyas (her sister Katie married into the Makhanyas. The CMMI has been registered as a nonprofit company (NPC).

Mme Charlotte's achievements and contributions to society both inside and beyond South Africa's borders motivated the families to seek recognition of her accomplishments as well as continue to promote her teachings, the values she stood for, and the continued empowering of women and social activism she pursued during her lifetime.

POLITICS

Francia Márquez via Earthjustice. "Francia Márquez, Renowned Afro-Colombian Activist: What Environmental Racism Means to Me." *Earthjustice* (blog). June 22, 2022. https://earthjustice.org/article/francia-m-rquez-renowned-afro-colombian-activist-what-environmental-racism-means-to-me.

BLACKNESS

Altheia Jones-LeCointe via *The Guardian*. "Altheia Jones-LeCointe: The Black Panther Who Became a Mangrove Nine Hero." September 9, 2021. Copyright Guardian News & Media Ltd, 2023. https://www.theguardian.com/society/2021/sep/09/altheia-jones-lecointe-the-black-panther-who-became-a-mangrove-nine-hero.

Katharina Oguntoye via Mathilde ter Heijne. "A Lot of Little Drops That Come Together to Make a Difference." April 26, 2019. https://www.terheijne.net/works/katharina-oguntoye.

Rosa Clemente (@rosaclemente). "Blackness is bigger than ethnicity, phenotype, or borders." Twitter. December 15, 2015. https://twitter.com/rosaclemente/status/676872312826626048.

Walter Rodney via the Walter Rodney Foundation. *The Groundings with My Brothers*. London: Bogle-Louverture, 1969.

PAN AFRICANISM

Horace Campbell. "Lessons from Wakanda: Pan-Africanism as the Antidote to Robotisation." *The Elephant*. May 24, 2018. https://www.theelephant.info/features/2018/05/24/lessons-from-wakanda-pan-africanism-as-the-antidote-to-robotisation.

Tiffany Pogue (@tiffanydphd). "Stop letting them test the family. Ya hear? Here's some homework so we can all do better." TikTok. November 22, 2022. https://tiktok.com/t/ZTREb1eqN.

BIBLIOGRAPHY

CULTURE AND HISTORY

Bourne, St. Clair, dir. *John Henrik Clarke: A Great and Mighty Walk*. New York: Black Dot Media, 1996.

Dwamena, Anakwa. "The Boundaries of the Global African Diaspora: An Interview with Marta Moreno Vega." *Africa Is a Country*. April 5, 2018. https://africasacountry.com/2018/04/the-boundaries-of-how-we-think-of-the-global-african-diaspora.

Equiano, Olaudah. *The Interesting Narrative of the Life of Olaudah Equiano, or Gustavus Vassa, the African. Written by Himself*. Self-published, 1789. https://docsouth.unc.edu/neh/equiano1/equiano1.html.

Harris, Kamala. "Remarks by Vice President Harris at a Political Event on Reproductive Rights." Delivered April 25, 2023. https://www.whitehouse.gov/briefing-room/speeches-remarks/2023/04/25/remarks-by-vice-president-harris-at-a-political-event-on-reproductive-rights.

Keetley, Dawn, and John Pettegrew, eds. *Public Women, Public Words: A Documentary History of American Feminism (Volume II: 1900 to 1960)*. Lanham, MD: Rowman & Littlefield Publishers, 2002.

Schomburg, Arturo Alfonso. Schomburg Center for Research in Black Culture, New York Public Library. Accessed June 8, 2023. https://www.nypl.org/locations/schomburg.

EDUCATION AND KNOWLEDGE

Bishop, Maurice. "Education Is a Must! Speech to Inaugurate the National In-Service Teacher Education Programme (NISTEP) at the Grenada Teacher's College, 30 October 1980," in *In Nobody's Backyard: Maurice Bishop's Speeches, 1979-1983*. London: Zed Books, 1984.

Du Bois, W.E.B. *The Souls of Black Folk*. Chicago: A.C. McClurg and Co., 1903. https://www.gutenberg.org/files/408/408-h/408-h.htm.

Hall, Prince. *A Charge, Delivered to the African Lodge, June 24, 1797, at Menotomy*. Boston: Benjamin Edes, 1797. https://quod.lib.umich.edu/e/evans/N24354.0001.001.

Selassie, Ermias Sable, ed. *The Wise Mind of Emperor Haile Selassie I*. Kingston, Jamaica: Miguel Lorne Publishers, 2002.

Williams, Talithia. *Power in Numbers: The Rebel Women of Mathematics*. Beverly, MA: Race Point Publishing, 2018.

JUSTICE, CIVIL RIGHTS, AND HUMAN RIGHTS

Bradford, Sarah H. *Scenes in the Life of Harriet Tubman*. Auburn, NY: W. J. Moses, 1869. https://docsouth.unc.edu/neh/bradford/bradford.html.

Fanon, Frantz. *Les damnés de la terre*. Paris: Éditions Maspero, 1961.

Jones, Barbara. "'I Don't Give a Damn What Anyone Thinks of Me': Winnie Mandela's Last Words in Final Fiery Interview Before She Died—Revealing the REAL Reason She and Nelson Split Up." *The Daily Mail*. Updated April 8, 2018. https://www.dailymail.co.uk/news/article-5590109/Winnie-Mandelas-words-final-interview-died-revealed-Nelson-split.html.

Terrell, Mary Church. "What It Means to Be Colored in the Capital of the US." Delivered October 10, 1906. https://www.blackpast.org/african-american-history/1906-mary-church-terrell-what-it-means-be-colored-capital-u-s.

Wells, Ida B. *Southern Horrors: Lynch Law in All Its Phases*. New York: New York Age Print, 1892. https://www.gutenberg.org/files/14975/14975-h/14975-h.htm.

RACE AND RACISM

Banneker, Benjamin. "To Thomas Jefferson from Benjamin Banneker, 19 August 1791." August 19, 1791. https://founders.archives.gov/documents/Jefferson/01-22-02-0049#TSJN-01-22-0049-an-0001.

MacKay, Claude. "Claude MacKay Describes His Own Life: A Negro Poet." *Pearson's Magazine*, vol. 38, no. 3 (1918): 275-276. http://www.marxisthistory.org/history/usa/groups/abb/1918/0900-mackay-hisownlife.pdf.

Smalls, Robert. "Historical Highlights: Representative Robert Smalls of South Carolina." Accessed June 8, 2023. https://history.house.gov/Historical-Highlights/1901-1950/Representative-Robert-Smalls-of-South-Carolina.

Valdivia, Angharad V. *A Latina in the Land of Hollywood: And Other Essays on Media*. Tucson: University of Arizona Press, 2000.

GENDER, FEMINISM, AND WOMANISM

Addy, E. A. *Ghana, A History for Primary Schools*. London: Longmans, Green and Co., 1958-1960.

Chisholm, Shirley. "I Am for the Equal Rights Amendment." Delivered August 10, 1970. https://www.blackpast.org/african-american-history/1970-shirley-chisholm-i-am-equal-rights-amendment.

Cooper, Anna Julia. *A Voice from the South*. Xenia, OH: The Aldine Printing House, 1892. https://docsouth.unc.edu/church/cooper/cooper.html.

Gates, Henry Louis, Jr. "Madam Walker, the First Black American Woman to Be a Self-Made Millionaire." Public Broadcasting System (PBS). June 2013. https://www.pbs.org/wnet/african-americans-many-rivers-to-cross/history/100-amazing-facts/madam-walker-the-first-black-american-woman-to-be-a-self-made-millionaire.

Jackson, Ketanji Brown. "Remarks by President Biden, Vice President Harris, and Judge Ketanji Brown Jackson on the Senate's Historic, Bipartisan Confirmation of Judge Jackson to Be an Associate Justice of the Supreme Court." Delivered April 8, 2022. https://www.whitehouse.gov/briefing-room/speeches-remarks/2022/04/08/remarks-by-president-biden-vice-president-harris-and-judge-ketanji-brown-jackson-on-the-senates-historic-bipartisan-confirmation-of-judge-jackson-to-be-an-associate-justice-of-the-supreme-court.

Pressley, Ayanna. "In Passionate Speech, Pressley Calls for Passage of Crown Act to Ban Hair Discrimination." Delivered March 18, 2022. https://pressley.house.gov/2022/03/18/passionate-speech-pressley-calls-passage-crown-act-ban-hair-discrimination.

PEACE AND LOVE

"bell hooks and Laverne Cox in a Public Dialogue at The New School." October 13, 2014. The New School. 1:36:08. CC BY 3.0 US. https://creativecommons.org/licenses/by/3.0/us. https://www.youtube.com/watch?v=9oMmZlJijgY.

Moore, William H. A. "Dusk Song." In *The Book of American Negro Poetry*, edited by James W. Johnson and compiled in 1922. Part of Lehigh University's "African American Poetry (1870-1927): A Digital Anthology," collected by Amardeep Singh. Updated January 10, 2022. https://scalar.lehigh.edu/african-american-poetry-a-digital-anthology/poems-by-william-ha-moore-included-in-the-book-of-american-negro-poetry-1922.

Sankara, Thomas. "Our White House Is in Black Harlem." Speech delivered in Harlem, New York, October 3, 1984. https://www.marxists.org/archive/sankara/1984/october/03.htm.

Walker, David. *Walker's Appeal, in Four Articles; Together with a Preamble, to the Coloured Citizens of the World, but in Particular, and Very Expressly, to Those of the United States of America, Written in Boston, State of Massachusetts, September 28, 1829*. Self-published, 1829. https://docsouth.unc.edu/nc/walker/walker.html.

Wheatley, Phillis. "Letter to Rev. Samson Occum." February 11, 1774. https://www.wheelersburg.net/Downloads/Wheatley%20and%20Adams%20Letters.pdf.

INSPIRATION, HOPE, AND PERSEVERANCE

Elliott, C. W. *St. Domingo: Its Revolutions, and Its Hero, Toussaint L'Ouverture, an Historical Discourse Condensed for the New York Library Association*. New York: J. A. Dix, 1855.

Gilbert, Olive. *Narrative of Sojourner Truth; a Bondswoman of Olden Time, Emancipated by the New York Legislature in the Early Part of the Present Century; with a History of Her Labors and Correspondence, Drawn from Her 'Book of Life.'* Self-published, 1850.

Johnson, James Weldon. "Lift Every Voice and Sing." New York: Edward B. Marks, 1900.

Kuitenbrouwer, Peter. "Remembering: Black-Rights Activist Dudley Laws." Published in the *National Post*, a division of Postmedia Network Inc. March 24, 2011. https://nationalpost.com/posted-toronto/remembering-black-rights-activist-dudley-laws.

FREEDOM AND LIBERATION

"Marching in the Arc of Justice Conference—Saturday Keynote: Opal [Ayọ] Tometi." March 7, 2015. Living Legacy Project. 52:35. CC BY 3.0 US: https://creativecommons.org/licenses/by/3.0/us. https://www.youtube.com/watch?v=a-D-6Wxzs7o.

Marsh, Charles. *God's Long Summer: Stories of Faith and Civil Rights*. Princeton, NJ: Princeton University Press, 2008.

Prince, Mary. *The History of Mary Prince, a West Indian Slave, Related by Herself*. London: F. Westley and A. H. Davis, 1831. https://docsouth.unc.edu/neh/prince/prince.html.

Riley, Charlotte Lydia. "'A People's Art is the Genesis of Their Freedom.'" *Tribune*. November 6, 2019. https://tribunemag.co.uk/2019/11/a-peoples-art-is-the-genesis-of-their-freedom.

"Samuel Sharpe." Jamaica Information Service. Accessed June 8, 2023. https://jis.gov.jm/information/heroes/samuel-sharpe.

Sedgwick, Catharine Maria. "Slavery in New England." *Bentley's Miscellany*, vol. 34 (1853): 417–424.

"Solomon Kalushi Mahlangu (1956–1979): The Order of Mendi for Bravery in Gold for Bravery and Sacrificing His Life for Freedom and Democracy in South Africa." Government of South Africa. https://www.gov.za/about-government/solomon-kalushi-mahlangu-1956-1979.

POLITICS

Douglass, Frederick. "Oration, Delivered in Corinthian Hall, Rochester, by Frederick Douglass, July 5th, 1852." Rochester, NY: Lee, Mann & Co., 1852. https://rbscp.lib.rochester.edu/2945.

Gibbs, Mifflin Wistar. *Shadow and Light: An Autobiography with Reminiscences of the Last and Present Century*. Self-published, 1902. https://www.gutenberg.org/files/28183/28183-h/28183-h.htm.

"Jesse Jackson in Portsmouth, NH 1988." Uploaded November 26, 2013. Eastern Video Productions. 4:41. CC BY 3.0 US. https://creativecommons.org/licenses/by/3.0/us. https://www.youtube.com/watch?v=rBEns-aD69Q.

"Minutes of an Interview Between the Colored Ministers and Church Officers at Savannah with the Secretary of War and Major-Gen. Sherman." *New-York Daily Tribune*. February 13, 1865. http://www.freedmen.umd.edu/savmtg.htm.

Obama, Barack. "Remarks by the President in Farewell Address." Delivered January 10, 2017. https://obamawhitehouse.archives.gov/the-press-office/2017/01/10/remarks-president-farewell-address.

BLACKNESS

Coleman, Anita Scott. "The Colorist." In *The Crisis*, 1925. Part of Lehigh University's "African American Poetry (1870–1927): A Digital Anthology," collected by Amardeep Singh. Updated August 5, 2022. https://scalar.lehigh.edu/african-american-poetry-a-digital-anthology/anita-scott-coleman-the-colorist-1925.

Johnson, James Weldon, ed. *The Book of American Negro Poetry*. New York: Harcourt, Brace and Company, Inc., 1922.

Jones, Electa F. *Stockbridge, Past and Present; or, Records of an Old Mission Station*. Springfield, MA: Samuel Bowles & Company, 1854. https://archive.org/stream/stockbridgepast00jonerich/stockbridgepast00jonerich_djvu.txt.

Stewart, Maria W. "Mrs. Stewart's Farewell Address to Her Friends in the City of Boston—Sept. 21, 1833." Delivered September 21, 1883. https://awpc.cattcenter.iastate.edu/2020/11/20/mrs-stewarts-farewell-address-to-her-friends-in-the-city-of-boston-sept-21-1833.

PAN AFRICANISM

Blyden, Edward Wilmot. "Africa's Service to the World." *The African Repository*, vol. 57, no. 8 (1881): 109–125.

Delany, Martin R. *The Condition, Elevation, Emigration, and Destiny of the Colored People of the United States*. Self-published, 1852. https://www.gutenberg.org/files/17154/17154-h/17154-h.htm.

Garvey, Amy Jacques. "Women as Leaders." *The Negro World*. October 25, 1925.

Harley, Sharon. "34. 'I Don't Pay Those Borders No Mind at All': Audley E. Moore ('Queen Mother' Moore)—Grassroots Global Traveler and Activist." In *Women and Migration: Responses in Art and History*. Edited by Deborah Willis, Ellyn Toscano, and Kalia Brooks Nelson. Cambridge, UK: Open Book Publishers, 2019. CC BY 4.0 US. https://creativecommons.org/licenses/by/4.0.

Sobukwe, Robert. "Robert Sobukwe Inaugural Speech, April 1959." Delivered April 1959. South African History Online. https://www.sahistory.org.za/archive/robert-sobukwe-inaugural-speech-april-1959.

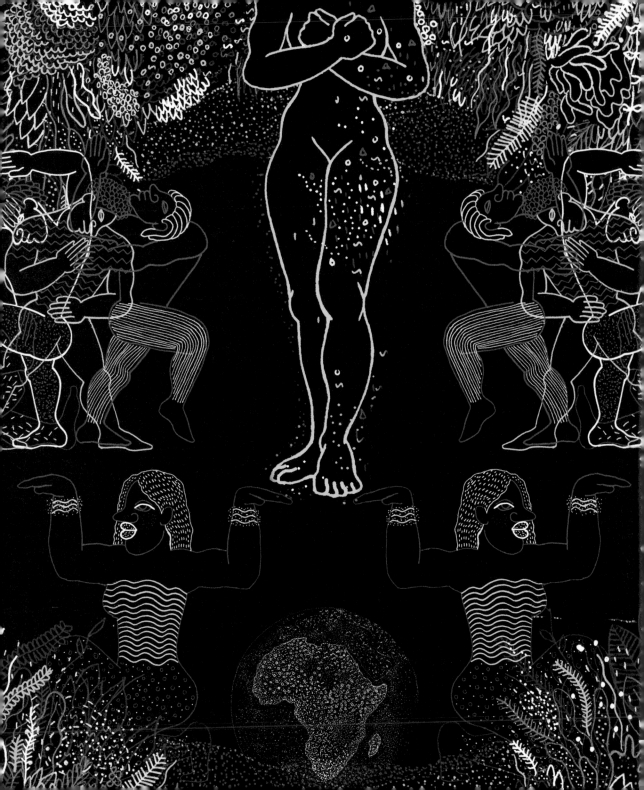

ABOUT THE AUTHOR

Jessica Ann Mitchell Aiwuyor is a cultural communications specialist based in the Washington, DC, area. Aiwuyor is the founder of the National Black Cultural Information Trust, a Pan African initiative that uses communications, media, and cultural storytelling to share information and resources that correct and challenge cultural misinformation and disinformation surrounding racial/ethnic identity, anti-Blackness, and other false narratives. Their work is centered on embracing collective cultural memories from the Black community and Pan African world as tools for education and solutions.

As an author and cultural storyteller, Aiwuyor has had writings about African American cultural heritage and ethnicity published and cited across a wide range of publications, including *Huffington Post, Business Insider*, MSNBC, *LA Progressive,* and TV One's *News One Now.* She publishes children's books celebrating Black life and culture with her publishing company, Our Legaci Press.

Instagram/X/TikTok: @jamaiwuyor

artist | Gilles Mayk Navangi, *Cosmos*

ABOUT THE ARTISTS

Affen Segun

Say It Out Loud IIII (p. 118)

Influenced by Black/African culture, Affen Segun's works explore the intersections of identity, representation, and sociopolitical behaviors of Africans. Drawing inspiration directly from his roots, Segun paints his subjects with a combination of ankara fabric and acrylic paints. His poetic visual language marries vibrantly colored, one-dimensional backgrounds with the expressive designs of the fabrics, commenting on the symbiotic correlation of the individual to their community. Transforming his own personal experiences and observations into the subjects in his paintings, he introduces viewers to the cultural diversity of Africa as well as its people and cultures.

Erin K. Robinson

Cover Art, *Dada Wazuri* (p. 6, 7), Untitled (p. 24–25), *Note to Self* (p. 40–41), *Aquarius* (p. 70, 71)

Erin K. Robinson is an Emmy-nominated illustrator whose work has been featured in the *New York Times, Washington Post,* and *O, The Oprah Magazine,* to name a few. She is also the illustrator for the children's books *A History of Me* (2022), *A Library* (2022), and *Brave. Black. First.* (2023). Robinson divides her time residing in Washington, DC, and Nairobi, Kenya. You can find her work on Instagram and her Etsy shop @Brooklyndolly.

Gilles Mayk Navangi

Elleux (p. 166), *Cosmos* (p. 188)

Gilles Mayk Navangi is a painter, illustrator, and sculptor. His work presents a dreamlike universe composed of graphic motifs, stylized vegetation, and human silhouettes that intermingle. He questions the representation of Black people today and is interested in various African traditions and civilizations, including ancient Egypt.

Nicole Collie

Father and Sons (p. 104, 105)

Nicole Collie would describe her work as Surrealism, with images that are celestial, ethereal, spiritual, and full of color and texture. Her art is her therapy that makes her mentally healthy. It represents the strength, majesty, and beauty of women and shows that they are incredible creatures able to do it all as mothers, lovers, caregivers, wives, friends, and teachers, and still have full-time jobs. Collie creates space for women to celebrate their bodies as much as they care for the world around them. Her paintings reflect mental health and beauty, inspiring women to see themselves as powerful and "imperfectly" perfect. Her website is www.nicolecollie.com.

Rendani Nemakhavhani

Noema Magazine (p. 54–55), *A WL Girlie* (p. 148, 149)

Based in South Africa, Rendani Nemakhavhani, also known as PR$DNT HONEY, is an illustrator, visual artist, and art director. She is interested and invested in telling and making stories that represent African people in a positive light and that pursue another narrative than the one given to us through the majority of media, prioritizing the portrayal of women. Her work exists in multiple mediums and is a reflection of where she is and how she thinks and interacts with the world. As a young and emerging artist, she is deeply influenced by the pursuit of creating an innovative, dynamic and postmodern graphic and visual vocabulary that redefines and questions the African identity and its perception.

Uzo Njoku

The Flower Man (p. 88), *My Black Perspective* (p. 134, 135)

Uzo Njoku is a versatile visual artist well known for her mesmerizing motifs used in her pattern making. Her colorful paintings which primarily depict melanated figures in different forms portray them in various contexts of beauty, all while incorporating her beautiful patterns in the paintings to create contrast and depth.

First published in 2024 by Wellfleet Press,
an imprint of The Quarto Group,
142 West 36th Street, 4th Floor, New York, NY 10018, USA
T (212) 779-4972 F (212) 779-6058 www.Quarto.com

Wellfleet Press titles are also available at discount for retail, wholesale, promotional, and bulk purchase. For details, contact the Special Sales Manager by email at specialsales@quarto.com or by mail at The Quarto Group, Attn: Special Sales Manager, 100 Cummings Center Suite 265D, Beverly, MA 01915 USA.

10 9 8 7 6 5 4 3 2 1

ISBN: 978-1-57715-377-1

Digital edition published in 2024
eISBN: 978-0-7603-8314-8

Library of Congress Cataloging-in-Publication Data

Names: Aiwuyor, Jessica Ann Mitchell, author.
Title: Black voices : inspiring & empowering quotes from global thought leaders / Jessica Ann Mitchell Aiwuyor.
Description: New York, NY : Wellfleet Press, 2024. | Includes bibliographical references. | Summary: "The ultimate compendium of empowering quotes from inspiring individuals across the African Diaspora, Black Voices features words of wisdom on topics from work to family, from activism to spirituality"— Provided by publisher.
Identifiers: LCCN 2023028690 (print) | LCCN 2023028691 (ebook) | ISBN 9781577153771 (hardcover) | ISBN 9780760383148 (ebook)
Subjects: LCSH: Black people—Quotations.
Classification: LCC PN6081.3 .A49 2024 (print) | LCC PN6081.3 (ebook) | DDC 080.8996—dc23/eng/20230802
LC record available at https://lccn.loc.gov/2023028690
LC ebook record available at https://lccn.loc.gov/2023028691

Group Publisher: Rage Kindelsperger
Editorial Director: Erin Canning
Creative Director: Laura Drew
Senior Art Director: Marisa Kwek
Managing Editor: Cara Donaldson
Editor: Elizabeth You
Cover and Interior Design: Angela Williams
Cover Art: Erin K. Robinson

Printed in China

Editor's Note: Throughout this book, the word "Black" has been capitalized when referencing a person or group of people. This choice has been made to respect the distinct culture and community across the Pan African world.